D1524939

XENOPHON'S PRINCE

XENOPHON'S PRINCE

Republic and Empire in the Cyropaedia

CHRISTOPHER NADON

UNIVERSITY OF CALIFORNIA PRESS
BERKELEY   LOS ANGELES   LONDON

The publisher gratefully acknowledges the generous contribution to this book provided by Joan Palevsky.

University of California Press
Berkeley and Los Angeles, California

University of California Press, Ltd.
London, England

An earlier version of the introduction was previously published as "From Republic to Empire: Political Revolution and the Common Good in Xenophon's Education of Cyrus," *American Political Science Review* 90, no. 2 (June 1996).

Library of Congress Cataloging-in-Publication Data

Nadon, Christopher, 1963–
    Xenophon's prince : republic and empire in the "Cyropaedia" / Christopher Nadon
       p.   cm.
    Includes bibliographical references and index.
    ISBN 0-520-22404-3 (cloth : alk. paper)
    1. Xenophon. Cyropaedia.   2. Cyrus, King of Persia, d. 529 B.C.—In literature.   3. Political fiction, Greek—History and criticism.   4. Politics and literature—Greece.   5. Imperialism—History—To 1500.   6. Republicanism in literature.
7. Imperialism in literature.   8. Republicanism—Greece.   9. Iran—In literature.   I. Title.
PA4494.C9 N33 2001
883'.01—dc21
                             00-055163

Manufactured in the United States of America
10 09 08 07 06 05 04 03 02 01
10 9 8 7 6 5 4 3 2 1
The paper used in this publication is both acid-free and totally chlorine-free (TCF).

To the memory of Allan Bloom
ἐκεῖνο δὲ κρίνω τοῦ ἀνδρὸς ἀγαστόν, τὸ τοῦ θανάτου παρεστηκότος μήτε τὸ φρόνιμον μήτε τὸ παιγνιῶδες ἀπολιπεῖν ἐκ τῆς ψυχῆς.

Il n'y a que les fols certains et resolus. "Che non men saper
dubbiar m'aggrada." *Car s'il embrasse les opinions de Xenophon
et de Platon par son propre discours, ce ne seront plus les leurs, ce
seront les siennes. Qui suit un autre, il ne suit rien. Il ne trouve
rien, voire il ne cherche rien.* "Non sumus sub rege; sibi quisque
se vindicet." *Qu'il sache qu'il sçait, au moins. Il faut qu'il emboive
leurs humeurs, non qu'il apprenne leurs preceptes.*

Montaigne, *Essais*, "De l'institution des enfans"

*For indeed if the question were, whether it were better to have
a particular act truly or faithfully set downe, there is no doubt
which is to be chosen, no more than whether you had rather have
Vespacians Picture right as he was, or at the Painters pleasure
nothing resembling. But if the question be for your owne use and
learning, whether it be better to have it set downe as it should be,
or as it was; then certainly is more doctrinable, the fained Cyrus
in Xenophon, then the true Cyrus in Justin.*

Philip Sidney, *Defense of Poesie*

Contents

Acknowledgments

I am grateful to the John M. Olin Foundation for supporting me during the time I devoted to writing this book. Wayne Ambler kindly provided me with a draft of his forthcoming translation and notes to the *Cyropaedia*. Karen Danford assisted me with translations from German.

Daniel Doneson, Stephen Gregory, Steve Lenzner, Christopher Lynch, Bipasa Nadon, Robert Nadon, and Patricia Thornton read and commented on various drafts. Ronald Spencer and Peter Dreyer exercised their considerable skills as copyeditors on the whole. It is hard for me to imagine a more thoughtful and helpful editor than Kate Toll of the University of California Press. The book is much better for their efforts.

As a student at the University of Chicago, I was fortunate to run up substantial debts to a number of talented teachers and scholars; among them, David Bolotin, François Furet, Amy Kass, Leon Kass, Ralph Lerner, Nathan Tarcov, Karl Weintraub, and Peter White. In his courses on the Hebrew Bible and medieval philosophy, Hillel Fradkin first impressed upon me the need to study politics. My greatest debt is to the late Allan Bloom. As a teacher, he showed great patience, generosity, and kindness and provided a model not only of how to read books but of how to live with and through them.

Abbreviations

Ages.	*Agesilaus*
Anab.	*Anabasis*
Apol.	*Apologia Socratis*
CL	*Constitution of the Lacedaemonians*
Cyn.	*Cynegeticus*
Cyro.	*Cyropaedia*
Hel.	*Hellenica*
Mem.	*Memorabilia*
Oec.	*Oeconomicus*
Symp.	*Symposium*

Introduction

The *Cyropaedia* as Political Theory

Xenophon is a peculiar case. Over the past 150 years, perhaps no other author from the classical tradition has been so little studied and so much reviled. In what was not so long ago considered the authoritative work on the subject, J. K. Anderson went so far as to conjure up for his readers the scene of a young Xenophon "hanging around the outskirts of a [Socratic] discussion, picking up something of the manner but not the matter." Had he been present, for instance, at the conversation recorded in Plato's *Laches*, "one might unkindly imagine Xenophon becoming bored and wandering off."[1] However unkind, this view does accurately reflect the dominant strains of nineteenth- and twentieth-century historical research, which claim to have uncovered not only Xenophon's lack of intelligence but his grave moral shortcomings as well. Among other things, he has been accused of "want of truthfulness as a man and patriotism as a citizen,"[2] and even denounced as a "hippie of the fourth century."[3] When *Xenophon the Athenian: The Problem of the Individual and the Society of the Polis* appeared in 1977, W. E. Higgins felt compelled by the reigning scholarly consensus to offer an apology simply for having written "a book about Xenophon *qua* Xenophon," that is, one that approached his works in a spirit of "critical humility" and with an appreciation of the Socratic irony with

---

1. Anderson 1974, 21. Vlastos 1991, 99, echoes this view: "One could hardly imagine a man who in taste, temperament, and critical equipment (or lack of it) would differ as much as did Xenophon from leading members of the inner Socratic circle."

2. Mure 1857, 3: 179.

3. Soulis 1972, 42.

1

which they are suffused.[4] His revisionist study traced the failure of
modern scholars to understand or appreciate Xenophon's works to an
initial and mistaken assumption about his manner of writing: "[They]
come to Xenophon all too often expecting a straightforward recital of
events such as they themselves might produce in a text or lecture." But
Xenophon, Higgins claims, is a playful master of understated parody, a
deft stylist who, "by saying 'what is not,' allusively summons forth 'what
is,'" and a dramatist who, by the careful juxtaposition of the words and
deeds of various characters, prompts his readers to see beneath the
surface of things and trains them to draw conclusions for themselves.[5]

As Higgins generously acknowledged, his approach owed much to
the work of Leo Strauss,[6] who was the first to question the premises and
presuppositions that led to the condemnation and neglect of Xenophon
in the nineteenth and twentieth centuries. In his study of the *Constitution of the Lacedaemonians,* Strauss made a persuasive case for the
high literary character of Xenophon's writings and argued that he took
a critical stance toward Sparta.[7] *On Tyranny*, his interpretation of the
Hiero, stands as a model of the care and concentration that must be
brought to bear when reading Xenophon's works.[8] Strauss's interests

4. Higgins 1977, xi, xii, 8.
5. Ibid., 2, 9, 13, 19–20.
6. Ibid., xiii.
7. Strauss 1939. For an appreciation of Leo Strauss's achievement, see Momigliano
1967, 1172. Much as Strauss did with Xenophon's *Constitution of the Lacedaemonians*,
Christopher Tuplin's study of the *Hellenica* debunks the commonly held belief in
Xenophon's pro-Spartan bias (Tuplin 1989, 31, 35, 41, 47, 62, 67, 72, 99, 165). Apart
from his substantive conclusions, Tuplin employs many hermeneutic principles similar
to Strauss's. Cf. Tuplin's discussion of the importance of "coded" or "implicit messages"
(121, 52, 108), the "decisive" character of arguments from silence or omission (84,
99, 149, 159), intentional contradictions (50, 76–77, 107–8, 161, 164), the frequent
use of irony, satire and parody (54, 125, 43, 98, 104–5, 177), and the justification for
such strategies in a plausible fear of persecution (167), with Strauss 1939 and 1968,
25–27, 40, 45, 46, 52–53, 56–57, 69, 71, 84, 86. Cf. also Tuplin's remarks on Proxenus
and Clearchus (162 n. 51) with Strauss 1983, 108–111. Not a single work by Strauss
appears in Tuplin's otherwise extensive bibliography. His explanation of Xenophon's
reticence might well account for his own.
8. Although a number of studies have recently appeared that recognize the need
to read Xenophon with something of the care and appreciation exemplified by Strauss
(Gray 1989, Riedinger 1991, Vander Waerdt 1994), his work is still widely ignored by
orthodox and establishment classicists. Pomeroy 1994, 24 n. 11, provides a revealing
explanation: "Strauss does not enjoy universal respect as a historian of philosophy.
Moreover, the fact that several of Strauss's disciples have been active in contemporary
conservative politics in the United States has complicated the 'Socratic problem' and

and concerns, however, were far from merely historical. Rather, he claimed that the study of Xenophon, particularly of his unusual mode of writing and the understanding of politics that dictated it, could provide an antidote to a kind of political fanaticism that Strauss traced to Rousseau, and, perhaps, correct what he regarded as the nineteenth century's pernicious misunderstanding of "the importance of the lowly art of rhetoric." Yet one need not accept such an expansive thesis to be reminded by Strauss of the indisputable fact that before the beginning of the nineteenth century, Xenophon was considered "a wise man and a classic in the precise sense."[9] If Higgins offers solace for the present state of affairs—"The sympathetic reader of Xenophon soon learns to savor the mutability of fortune"[10]—Strauss encourages us to reflect on the remarkable stability of Xenophon's reputation over the centuries and to wonder whether it can simply be ascribed to luck. When Milton praises "the divine volumes of Plato and his equal Xenophon,"[11] he expresses the judgment of a variety of classical authors, among them Polybius, Cicero, Tacitus, Dionysius of Halicarnassus, Quintilian, Aulus Gellius, and Longinus, who likewise ranked him among the best of philosophers and historians.[12] In Renaissance and early modern times, Alberti, Castiglione, Montaigne, Montesquieu, Rousseau, Bacon, Spenser, Swift, Bolingbroke, Shaftesbury, Gibbon, and Franklin all concurred with the classical view. Moreover, Xenophon's works have been preserved over the centuries in their entirety, and this without the benefit of special care from any particular school, a compliment rarely paid to so prolific an author. Although he laments their efforts, even Anderson admits that "many scribes, and their employers, in many generations, thought his works worth copying out."[13] One cannot help but wonder at the disparity between the old view and our own.

---

caused some other scholars to give short shrift to Straussian interpretations of Greek philosophy." See also, Pomeroy 1996; cf. Ferrari 1997, 36–39.

9. Strauss 1968, 24–27.

10. Higgins 1977, 1.

11. Milton, *Prose Writings*, 70; cf. Gibbon 1994, 2: 610.

12. For a list and analysis of references to Xenophon in the classical sources, see Tuplin 1993, 21–28.

13. Anderson 1974, 8.

Rediscovering the *Cyropaedia*

Xenophon was among the most widely read authors in antiquity, and the *Cyropaedia* was considered his masterpiece.[14] When classical learning revived in Europe, his works were among the first carried back from Byzantium. In the fifteenth century, the *Cyropaedia* was especially sought after and studied, interest in it likely piqued by its reputation as a favorite of both Scipio and Caesar.[15] A similar consensus as to the importance of the *Cyropaedia* in Xenophon's corpus is emerging today, as witnessed by the recent publication of three book-length studies: Bodil Due's *The Cyropaedia: Xenophon's Aims and Methods*; James Tatum's *Xenophon's Imperial Fiction*; and Deborah Levine Gera's *Xenophon's Cyropaedia: Style, Genre, and Literary Technique*.[16] All three authors make a persuasive case that Xenophon's writings demand a more serious philosophical and literary analysis than conventionally considered, and they come to remarkably similar conclusions as to Xenophon's overall intention in the work. Yet to read these three books together is to be struck by the different and ultimately contradictory paths their authors take to arrive at such agreement. The character of the problem this creates can be brought out most concisely by focusing on each one's treatment of the last chapter of the *Cyropaedia*, wherein Xenophon describes the swift collapse of the empire Cyrus founded and the moral degeneracy of his descendants. All three agree that the controversial epilogue provides the key to deciphering the meaning of the *Cyropaedia* and consider the ability to explain its inclusion in the work to be the test of the soundness of any interpretation.

Bodil Due gives the most straightforward account of the *Cyropaedia*. She claims that Xenophon wished to present the portrait of an "ideal ruler" in order to provide a model for imitation by his contemporaries.[17] The utility of such a work follows from Xenophon's

14. Munscher 1920, 24.

15. Cicero *Ep. ad Quint.* 1.1.23; Suetonius *Jul.* 87. For a brief *nachleben* of the *Cyropaedia* in Renaissance Italy, see Sancisi-Weerdenburg 1990, 31–52. See Tatum 1989, 3–35, for a fuller account that covers France and England.

16. See also the entry for Xenophon in the most recent edition of the *Oxford Classical Dictionary* (1996): "The *Cyropaedia* has been found dull in modern times. But a revival of interest is underway, and it is arguably a litmus-test for a true appreciation of Xenophon in general."

17. Due 1989, 25, 234.

view that "without the highest possible moral standards in the leader—and a leader there must be in a state, as well as in an army or a family—there is no hope of improving the sad and confused conditions of human life."[18] It therefore comes as no surprise that, according to Due, Xenophon thought that the good leader was a virtuous one. To confirm this view, she refers to Xenophon's descriptions of Cyrus's "kindness, clemency and concern for other people, combined with strength, discipline, and capacity for endurance in both a moral as well as physical sense." She also makes much of Cyrus's "generosity and natural deportment towards his men."[19] In short, Cyrus represents the perfection of the conventional human virtues. Given her laudatory presentation, Due knows that it may dispirit or shock some readers to learn that the empire founded by this ideal ruler collapsed immediately upon his death. Is this not a severe reproach to the skill and judgment of its founder, one that casts doubts on the solidity of Cyrus's virtues and foresight? Due denies that Xenophon could have wished to detract from his portrait of Cyrus by including the account of his empire's sad fate. Rather, Due claims, "by implicit contrast, he succeeds in underlining, for the last time, the exceptional nature of Cyrus. . . . Thus the first and the last chapter form a circle or train of thoughts around the whole work. The only way to avoid such a [miserable] state of affairs is to have a perfect leader."[20] The strength of Due's argument derives from its simplicity, which in turn leaves the unity of Xenophon's vision and intention wholly intact.[21]

Due intends her book to provide not only an interpretation of the *Cyropaedia* but also a vindication of Xenophon's worth before a community of scholars that has either disparaged or ignored him. Accordingly, she writes with the passion of someone moved by the sight of injustice, a passion she freely admits may sometimes get the better of

18. Ibid., 237, 19.
19. Ibid., 37, 232.
20. Ibid., 19.
21. W. E. Higgins also stresses Xenophon's intention to present Cyrus as an ideal and exemplary ruler, particularly in his respect for justice (Higgins 1977, 47–48, 53–55, 57–58, 65). And, like Bodil Due, he thinks the last chapter is designed to show that "when the great man is gone, the society crumbles" (57). One should note, however, that this interpretation of the *Cyropaedia* is significantly modified in the later chapters of his study (125–26).

her judgment.[22] This seems to have happened on at least one occasion where, to defend Xenophon against criticism of his talents as a writer, she finds herself forced to deny that politics is even in the realm, much less in the forefront, of his concerns: "The vagueness and ambiguity as regards the nature of Cyrus's power is not, I think, clumsiness on the part of Xenophon, but originates from lack of interest."[23] Due clearly admires Xenophon above all as a literary stylist and therefore considers vagueness, ambiguity, and clumsiness in composition to be sins much less forgivable than inattention to or lack of interest in politics.[24] But this is demonstrably not Xenophon's view. A glance at the titles of his works, to say nothing of their contents, confirms the centrality of politics to Xenophon's interests; and his Socrates sometimes takes others to task for their neglect of political life as both a practical and a theoretical concern.[25] We might wonder, then, whether in attempting to establish what she considers the enduring literary beauty and value of the *Cyropaedia*, Due goes too far in idealizing or purifying Cyrus's virtues, thus giving us a portrait that lacks the hard edge and nuances of Xenophon's own presentation. Indeed, on the basis of her bland, if sunny, characterization of Cyrus's moral perfections, it is impossible to imagine how the book could have held such fascination for thinkers of the subtlety of Cicero, Milton, or Montaigne, to say nothing of the power it exercised over military men like Alexander, Caesar, Gustavus, and Wolfe. Such, at any rate, is the kind of objection James Tatum would likely offer Due, for by entering into the political dimensions that she explicitly dismisses, he finds a Cyrus who possesses both moral and immoral "virtues."

The Cyrus that James Tatum presents in *Xenophon's Imperial Fiction* is a fitting object of study for Xenophon's best-known and most devoted reader, Machiavelli.[26] This Cyrus treats those around him only as useful tools, to be manipulated for his own ends, and makes so little

22. Due 1989, 9–10, 230.
23. Ibid., 25.
24. Due's standards are explicitly literary or esthetic: "I propose to . . . demonstrate that [Xenophon] was an able artist and mastered his subject with style and elegance. . . . It is one of the aims of the present study to try to understand the inspiration that emanated from this book and to try to re-instate it with regard to its literary value" (ibid., 9–10).
25. E.g., *Mem.* 1.1.11–16, 2.1ff.
26. Tatum 1989, 8.

distinction between family, friends, and foes that Tatum can describe his mother and grandfather as among "his first victims."[27] Furthermore, Tatum claims, "he is ruthlessly self-serving and subversive of the status-quo," willing "to bend the laws and customs of the Persians to his own interest," and ready "to abandon the norms of one society for another when it suits his purposes." Among the many less than wholesome purposes Tatum detects, foremost is to submit the government of the world to his own will. As we might gather from this list, Cyrus cannot be suspected of harboring any "simple piety."[28] The *Cyropaedia*'s modern reputation as "a tedious moral fiction," a view only reinforced by Due's account, crumbles beneath the weight of Tatum's observations.

Perhaps more shocking than this accurate, if incomplete, catalogue of Cyrus's less than reputable qualities is Tatum's firm and often repeated agreement with Due that Cyrus nevertheless represents the "paradigm of the ideal ruler," one whose "positive example" is intended by Xenophon to provide a model for imitation.[29] The suspicion that Tatum considers both Xenophon and his Cyrus ruthless Machiavellians some two thousand years *avant la lettre*,[30] and, moreover, that he approves of this position today, is heightened by his bringing together on the same page Xenophon's claim that Cyrus enjoyed the "willing obedience" of his subjects with a description of them "obeying out of terror." This juxtaposition moves Tatum to conclude, "Here is the ideal leader, and the reason why we want to study him."[31] Does neither Xenophon nor Tatum differentiate between consent freely given and that compelled by unlawful force? Several passages from the *Memorabilia* reassure us that Xenophon did in fact distinguish between tyranny and kingship,[32] and Tatum goes on to uncover evidence within the *Cyropaedia* itself to show that Xenophon also disapproved of rule by terror. According to Tatum, the "supremely bad" Assyrians are

27. Ibid., 66, 68, 97, 71, 115; cf. 83, 87.
28. Ibid., 98, 71, 218, 106, 86.
29. Ibid., xv, 37, 62, 68, 233.
30. Ibid., 66, "[S]o long as we regard everyone Cyrus meets as a person to be controlled, as someone potentially useful for the future course of his empire, we shall be of the same mind as Cyrus and the writer who created him."
31. Ibid., 62–63.
32. E.g., *Mem.* 4.6.12, 3.2.2.

Cyrus's "dialectical opposites," and their king "provides a nice example
of the futility of attempting to rule an empire by terror." Deploying an
all-too-familiar political syllogism, Tatum concludes that since Cyrus
ultimately defeats this incarnation of evil, he cannot himself be bad.[33]

It remains, then, for Tatum to explain how these harsher, less prin-
cipled sides of Cyrus can be reconciled with his claim that Xenophon
considered him an ideal ruler. While admitting that some of the more
disreputable aspects of Cyrus's behavior might provide instruction
about certain unavoidable if unpleasant political necessities,[34] Tatum
denies their essential contribution to the narrative. What is most important is that by the end of the book, Cyrus comes out altogether
clean. "If there are any sinister aspects to Cyrus's rise to power, they
disappear with the death of Panthea and Abradatas. From the moment
Babylon falls and the evil Assyrian [king] is slain, the world of the *Cyropaedia* is a radiant and happy place with not a villain in sight." Tatum
agrees with Due that Cyrus's achievement "would amount to very little
if he did not change the world for the better."[35] Yet this leaves him
with the same difficulty faced by Due. If the mature Cyrus is so good
and his empire ideal, why does it fall so quickly and inflict such lasting
damage on its subjects?

Tatum has little patience for those who would dodge this problem by
the simple expedient of denying that Xenophon wrote the chapter that
describes that fall. He accepts Gustav Eichler's strictly philological arguments for the authenticity of the so-called epilogue.[36] But whereas
Eichler wished to discourage speculation about the actual meaning
of the chapter,[37] Tatum insists on pursuing the issue on substantive
grounds to determine "what this ending reveals about the connections
between what Xenophon created and actual political experience."[38]
Some aspects of his explanation coincide with Due's. To the extent
that Cyrus is an "ideal prince," Tatum recognizes that the swift collapse of his empire could be taken as a reproach. But, like Due, he
finds that "the focus here is really more on [the decadence of] Cyrus's

33. Tatum 1989, 93–94.
34. Ibid., 188.
35. Ibid.,188–89.
36. Ibid., 221–24.
37. Eichler 1880, 87.
38. Tatum 1989, 225.

descendants and contemporary Persia than on the text of the *Cyropae-dia*." The comparison is intended to work in Cyrus's favor, to show the key importance of his leadership.[39] But Tatum also wishes to develop a further, more elaborate point. He claims that the inconsistencies between the body of Xenophon's text and its surprising ending are real. Yet this does not mean that the epilogue is an interpolation by some later writer. Rather, these inconsistencies reflect fundamental equivocations that Xenophon experienced over the long course of writing the *Cyropaedia* in his attitude toward the text and its hero. According to Tatum, Xenophon was a gifted dramatist, capable of transforming a few bare scraps of history into an "ideal fiction," a "romantic world" where perfect virtue always triumphs.[40] But he was also a hard-nosed political thinker and historian who took his bearings from the facts.[41] Ultimately, the worldly pressures and disappointments that pushed Xenophon toward writing fiction in the first place "impinge on the perfected world that he creates through Cyrus."[42] Thus, "the gap between the political and historical world of the *Cyropaedia* finally outweighed his authorial desire to preserve the integrity of the text he created *Contradictory strategies and mutually exclusive points of view* exist side by side at many places in his writings."[43] The contradiction between the book as a whole and its last chapter thus finds its deepest source in the incoherence of Xenophon's mind, torn as it was between reality and fiction:

> The gap between the perfections of Cyrus and all the imperfections of present day Persia is so great the fantasy cannot continue. The result is discordant ... the problems the *Cyropaedia* addresses are inescapably privileged by reality. Therein [Xenophon] discovers another kind of irony. Just as he records how Cyrus, Agesilaus, Epaminondas, and even he himself embarked on one project in life and ended up in ways none of them could foresee, so now he discovers that even the writing of fiction can be as much subject to revision as any other kind of text.[44]

39. Ibid., 220, 37.
40. Ibid., 216, xiv, 189.
41. Ibid., 237.
42. Ibid., 238.
43. Ibid., 224, emphasis added. See also 234, and the implicit subordination of Xenophon to his creation: "[T]he original vision of the author transforms itself into something contrary to what he began with."
44. Ibid., 238.

Yet the "revision" Tatum ascribes to Xenophon is nothing like the kind
of rewrite such fundamental inconsistencies and contradictions would
call for were he to receive a passing grade on a midterm examination.
It is instead a hasty postscript recanting most of the previous two
hundred pages. In this way, Tatum manages to save the authority
of the text, but only at the expense of its author. This is not a loss
that he has any cause to regret, for in his view, "dialectical scrutiny
of the principles people think they live by is something in which
[Cyrus] does not care to indulge. So far as we can tell, neither did
the author who created him."[45] *Xenophon's Imperial Fiction* presents
an unconventional argument leading to the conventional valuation of
Xenophon's ultimate worth. Or, to borrow Cyrus's image of Median
culinary excess, Tatum takes an indirect and winding path only to
arrive at the same judgment that others have long since and more
simply reached.

Deborah Levine Gera's *Xenophon's Cyropaedia: Style, Genre, and
Literary Technique* is above all a study of the literary influences that
have left their traces on Xenophon's book. As such, it is a comprehen-
sive and sensitive guide to Xenophon's possible sources and is particularly illuminating on the extensive and imaginative use he made of
Herodotus's *Histories*.[46] But Gera goes well beyond the mere compila-
tion and comparison of sources. She recognizes that the greatest merit
of the *Cyropaedia* lies in its "contribution to the political theory of
[Xenophon's] own time," and, accordingly, devotes the final chapter
of her study to a consideration of "Xenophon's attitude toward his
hero" and what it reveals about the meaning of the book.[47] Gera, too,
focuses on the problematic relationship between the epilogue and all
that comes before it as the key to understanding Xenophon's intention.

Like Tatum and Due, Gera takes Xenophon's Cyrus to be "a model
to others who wish to cultivate virtue," an "ideal ruler" who turns out to
be "a kind of philosopher king."[48] On the whole, he is "wise, virtuous,
and ever successful in achieving his ambitions," even while remain-

---

45. Ibid., 39.
46. See also Tatum 1989, 147–57, for what he calls the "intertextuality" of the
Cyropaedia and Herodotus's *Histories*.
47. Gera 1993, 13, vi.
48. Ibid., 7, 122, cf. 284.

ing "a zealous guardian of the property of others."[49] Yet Gera, like Tatum, detects another side to Cyrus. She notes that "his seemingly kind and thoughtful policies are consistently shown to be motivated by utilitarian, if not selfish, considerations," and that he practices a disquieting policy of "divide and conquer" against his *friends*. Moreover, he confiscates the property of his allies, curries popular favor using methods typical of tyrants, and in the end resembles no one so much as his grandfather Astyages, the lawless, "self-aggrandizing" despot of Media. Gera even suggests that we take Cyrus's well-known epithet, "Shepherd of the People," in a Thrasymachean rather than Homeric sense.[50] Indulging in a bit of Xenophontic understatement herself, she remarks that "each of the less than ideal features of Cyrus's behavior as a ruler of an empire, taken by itself, is perhaps no more than slightly disquieting; viewed cumulatively, they are disturbing and require some sort of explanation."[51]

Gera's own explanation runs as follows. The overarching lesson Xenophon wishes to teach in the *Cyropaedia* is that "both benevolence and despotism are needed to run a large empire successfully." The first corollary of this major premise is that one must choose between "the careful and virtuous republic of a small-scale polity and the more extensive, but despotic, empire." It follows, then, that "the second consequence of Cyrus's enlightened absolutism is that it must in fact be enlightened." What she means by this apparent tautology is that the institutions and way of life Cyrus creates are themselves insufficient to sustain the empire without his skillful guidance.[52] Persian decadence is not the result of abandoning the practices instituted by Cyrus; it is their fruit. From this she draws the conclusion that "the despotism he inaugurates is what is left to the following generations of Persians— along with the conquered empire—and it is a poor legacy. The epilogue only serves to confirm this point, if in an extreme and outspoken way."[53] Here, Gera takes us to the point of a possible breach between Xenophon and his Cyrus. Her understanding of his intention in the final chapter forces us to ask, not only whether Xenophon approved

49. Ibid., 280, 222.
50. Ibid., 294, 298, 290, 293, 295.
51. Ibid., 296.
52. Ibid., 297–98.
53. Ibid., 298.

or disapproved of how Cyrus organized and ruled his empire, but, more fundamentally, whether he thought his hero's choice of empire over republic sound. Indeed, the movement from republic to empire obliges the reader to consider which Xenophon preferred and, more important, to elucidate the grounds of that preference. In other words, the *Cyropaedia* raises, albeit in a subdued or indirect manner, the central question of classical political philosophy: "What is the best regime?" True to her stress on the *Cyropaedia* as a work of political theory, Gera's study shows why it properly belongs in the tradition of regime analysis more usually associated with Plato and Aristotle.

Gera fails to pursue the more radical implications of her analysis, however, and ultimately comes to two separate and contradictory conclusions. First, she claims that the collapse brought on by the character of Cyrus's empire shows that he instituted practices "which cannot be considered, either by the author himself or by his readers, ideal." There is thus "a certain distance or tension in this final section of the work between Xenophon and his hero."[54] But, second, this same collapse serves to demonstrate "how much better [Cyrus] was than present day Persians." Like Tatum and Due, she takes Xenophon's last chapter to be yet another rhetorical device or literary technique "to idealize Cyrus."[55] This unsettled conclusion, that Xenophon both loves and does not love his Cyrus, turns out to be another way of expressing Tatum's thesis on the ambiguity of the relation between the artist and his creation. It goes without saying that Gera, too, ends by asserting the essential incoherence of Xenophon's work.

By focusing on the political dimensions of the *Cyropaedia*, Tatum and Gera manage to elicit a depth and complexity lacking in Due's account, and they reach a noteworthy agreement concerning both the meaning and merit of the book. Yet what is most striking in the comparison of their studies is not the similarity of their conclusions, but

54. Ibid., 299.
55. Ibid., 300. Christian Mueller-Goldingen (1995, 263) likewise considers the comparison between past and present to work entirely in Cyrus's favor and notes the parallel to Xenophon's treatment of Lycurgus in chapter 14 of the *Constitution of the Lacedaemonians*. Further, "Xenophon wishes to show that it is not the institutions Cyrus founded, nor the customs he promoted, but rather his successors who are responsible for the decline. This conforms to the utmost with the conviction already expressed in the proem, that Cyrus achieved something unique with his rule" (264–65). But for the ambiguity of Cyrus's uniqueness, see Sage 1994, 164–65.

the different paths they take to arrive at them. Tatum finds several aspects of Cyrus's childhood and rise to power disturbing, but he is altogether satisfied with the ideal character of the empire he founds: it is "a radiant and happy place without a villain in sight."[56] Gera, conversely, is relatively pleased with Xenophon's Cyrus up until the point when he founds his empire. The abuses she documents are almost all taken from the final sections of the work. Moreover, whereas Tatum is reassured as to Cyrus's ultimate goodness by his victory over the "evil Assyrian," Gera documents troubling similarities between Cyrus and his archenemy.[57] The fact that where Tatum sees good, Gera sees bad, and where Gera sees good Tatum sees bad, suggests the possibility that Xenophon and his presentation of Cyrus are in fact consistent throughout the work, indeed, consistently "Machiavellian." On this subject, we are fortunate in that Machiavelli left an extensive record of his views.

Machiavelli's Cyrus

Before the recovery of classical learning and the reintroduction of the *Cyropaedia*, Cyrus the Great was apparently known to Europeans primarily from various accounts derived from that found in Herodotus's *Histories*.[58] Dante, Petrarch, and Boccaccio all refer to Cyrus as a rapacious king who met a fitting if gruesome end at the hands of Queen Tomyris. His name seems to have been proverbial for that of a wicked king.[59] With the diffusion and translation of Xenophon's *Cyropaedia* in the fifteenth century, this reputation began to change.[60] Cyrus now appeared in a number of "mirrors of princes" as an ideal ruler. Giovanni Pontano, for example, considered him "a model not only of justice but of all the virtues of a ruler," and praised him for his liberality, devotion to friendship, and truthfulness.[61] In Platina's *De Principe*, Cyrus appears as a paradigm of piety and benevolence,

56. Tatum 1989, 189.
57. Gera 1993, 285, 287–96, 112.
58. Sancisi-Weerdenburg 1990, 33–35.
59. Dante, *Purgatorio*, 12.55–57; *De Monarchia*, 2.8. Boccaccio, *Ameto* (in *Literatura italiana* 8), 903, 1211. Petrarch, "Trionfi della Pudicizia," 104–5; "Trionfi della Fama," 2.94–99.
60. For the history of the Greek codices and early translations of the *Cyropaedia*, see Voigt 1888, Sabbadini, 1905.
61. Pontano 1952, 1024, 1028, 1040.

illustrating the difference between a meritorious ruler and a tyrant.[62] Leon Battista Alberti frequently counseled imitation of Cyrus for the proper management of one's household.[63] And in *Il libro del Cortegiano*, Baldassare Castiglione explicitly set out to imitate Xenophon and pronounced his Cyrus to be "a perfect king."[64] When Machiavelli came to rank Cyrus among the most excellent men who had become princes by reason of their own virtue and not by fortune, he seems, then, to have been following in the new civic-humanist tradition. But Machiavelli was rarely, if ever, content simply to follow in the footsteps of others.[65] His understanding and use of Cyrus prove no exception to this rule.

Machiavelli first mentions Cyrus in chapter 6 of the *Prince*, where he figures with Moses, Romulus, and Theseus as one of the "greatest examples" held up for admiration and imitation.[66] Given the laudatory presentation, we might assume that Machiavelli has in mind the good Cyrus of the *Cyropaedia* rather than the savage king of Herodotus's *Histories*. But this would be a mistake. For Machiavelli goes on in chapter 6 to discuss how Cyrus would never have succeeded without the necessary *occasione* of finding "the Persians malcontent with the empire of the Medes, and the Medes soft and effeminate because of the long peace."[67] This description is entirely in keeping with what Herodotus relates about the political situation on the eve of Cyrus's conquests, and it is very difficult to square with the account given in the *Cyropaedia*, where the Persians and Medes appear instead as allies united against the Assyrian aggressor.[68]

Whatever ambiguity remains about whether Machiavelli is referring to the Cyrus of Herodotus or of Xenophon in chapter 6, in chapter 14, he explicitly settles on the latter. There, Machiavelli advises the prince to exercise his mind by reading histories in which the actions of excellent men are recorded:

62. Platina, *De Principe*, 57, 72, 172, 55.
63. Alberti, *Opere volgari*, 1: 313, 331, 336.
64. Castiglione, *Il libro del cortegiano*, 12, 73, 317–18.
65. Machiavelli, *Discourses*, Preface. For Machiavelli's reservations about the Renaissance commonplace that princes should imitate the lives of excellent men, see Macfarland 1999, 145.
66. Machiavelli, *Prince*, 22.
67. Ibid., 23.
68. Compare Herodotus 1.123–30 with *Cyro.* 1.4; 1.5; 1.6.10.

Above all he should do as some excellent man has done in the past who found someone to imitate who had been praised and glorified before him, whose exploits and actions he always kept beside himself, as they say Alexander the Great imitated Achilles; Caesar, Alexander; Scipio, Cyrus. And whoever reads the life of Cyrus written by Xenophon will then recognize how much glory that imitation brought him, and how much in chastity, affability, humanity, and liberality Scipio conformed to what had been written of Cyrus by Xenophon.[69]

The reference to the *Cyropaedia* not only appears to confirm that Machiavelli has Xenophon's Cyrus in mind, it also indicates that he adheres to the civic-humanist reading of the book. What makes Cyrus worthy of imitation is his chastity, affability, humanity, and liberality. Still, it is worth noting that when Machiavelli explicitly refers to Xenophon's Cyrus, he does not counsel direct imitation, as he seemed to do in chapter 6. Rather, a prince "should do as some excellent man has done in the past who found someone to imitate who had been praised and glorified before him," Strictly speaking, this means that he should imitate, not Achilles or Cyrus, but rather their imitators, Alexander and Scipio. A prince should *be* like Caesar, who in imitating an imitator actually conforms to the letter of Machiavelli's advice. This preference for Caesar over Cyrus prepares the way for the strong re-buke he levels in the next chapter against Xenophon and other writers like him. Having just encouraged us to read the *Cyropaedia*—a work that contains an account of an imaginary republic and principality— Machiavelli continues, "But since my intent is to write something useful to whoever understands it, it has appeared to me more fitting to go directly to the effectual truth of the thing than to the imagination of it. And many have imagined republics and principalities that have never been seen or known to exist in truth; for it is so far from how one lives to how one should live that he who lets go of what is done for what should be done learns his ruin rather than his preservation."[70] In the chapters immediately following this declaration of intent, Machiavelli turns against that most assiduous reader of Xenophon and imitator of Cyrus, Scipio.

Scipio, it turns out, serves as Machiavelli's primary example of the kind of ruin to be expected when a prince tries to follow the

69. Machiavelli, *Prince*, 60.
70. Ibid., 61.

admonitions of "the writers." As a result of the "excessive mercy" and "agreeable nature" he cultivated out of esteem for Xenophon's Cyrus, Scipio failed to maintain sufficient discipline among his soldiers, and the armies in Spain rebelled. This breakdown threatened to corrupt the Roman military. All that saved Scipio and Rome was the good fortune of being subject to the Roman Senate, whose members could reprove his mercy and hide the "damaging quality" of his agreeable nature, which otherwise "would in time have sullied his fame and glory."[71] It would have been much better for him to be like Hannibal, a general whose "inhuman cruelty ... together with his infinite virtues" allowed him to lead a very large army made up of different kinds of men without the least dissension, "in bad as well as good fortune." Machiavelli does offer something of an excuse for Scipio's weakness. He was, after all, only following the example set by Cyrus. The real fault, then, seems to lie with Xenophon and other "writers" who give idealistic accounts of the kind of virtues a prince should exercise. Even worse, while they admire political success, they actually condemn the harsh but necessary qualities that are "the principle cause of it," for example, Hannibal's inhuman cruelty.[72] Instead of recording what Cyrus must have done in order to succeed, Xenophon, in his naivety, imagined rather what he thought a good prince ought to do. He thereby misled Scipio as to the kind of duties imposed by the necessities faced by real generals and statesmen.

A cursory comparison of the "historical" Cyrus found in the *Histories* with the imaginative fiction of the *Cyropaedia* bears out this charge. According to Herodotus, Cyrus's Median grandfather tried to have him exposed at birth, a favor Cyrus later returned by leading a rebellion of the Persians in which the old man was overthrown and made prisoner.[73] According to Xenophon, Cyrus and Astyages were on quite friendly terms. The grandfather died a natural death well before Cyrus came to power; and the kingdom of the Medes descended to the latter by marriage, not conquest.[74] Even more striking are the different accounts of Cyrus's death. In the *Histories*, Cyrus fell in battle, and his head

71. Ibid., 68.
72. Ibid., 67.
73. Herodotus 1.73–75, 127–30.
74. *Cyro.* 1.3–4; 1.5; 8.5.19–20.

was chopped off and plunged into a bucket of human blood so that he might at last have his fill of gore.[75] According to Xenophon, Cyrus met his death in bed, surrounded by friends and family and well advanced in age.[76] The contrast between the two could hardly be more complete, or Xenophon's version more misleading as to the cruel necessities and dangers of actual political life. Discrepancies such as these appear to be characteristic of Xenophon's improved or sanitized version of Cyrus's life. In his world, the virtues, perfected in the character of Cyrus, always seem to triumph. But for Machiavelli, this naivety, however charming or reassuring to conventional morality, makes the *Cyropaedia* a kind of fairy tale, a work perhaps more fit for the entertainment of children than the instruction of princes.[77] Moreover, the argument of chapter 15 of the *Prince* implies that this apparent hopefulness about morality is in fact quite dangerous, because it always threatens to transform itself into an inflexible, if high minded, political idealism. In practice, Xenophon and those who write like him disarm decent men who follow the conventional strictures they espouse, but leave the wicked untouched and therefore more likely to prevail without real or well-organized opposition. Machiavelli therefore rejects this Cyrus as an example fit for the imitation of princes, and his author as a model of good or effective writing. Accordingly, when he exhorts the reader in the final chapter of the *Prince* "to learn the greatness of the spirit of Cyrus," he returns to the Cyrus of Herodotus.[78] The hard-nosed Machiavelli prefers history to fiction.[79]

One could perhaps rest satisfied with this understanding of the grounds for Machiavelli's rejection of Xenophon's Cyrus, and those

75. Herodotus 1.212–14.

76. *Cyro.* 8.7.

77. Wheeler 1962 maintains that the *Cyropaedia* is in fact the founding document of the genre of children's literature.

78. The descriptions of Cyrus's *occasione* in *The Prince*, chs. 6 and 26, are similarly Herodotean.

79. This preference, if based on rather different grounds, for a historical figure over Xenophon's imagined ideal was expressed as early as 1461 by Donato Acciaiuoli in the Dedication of his *Life of Charlemagne*: "I see it as a duty to write about [Charlemagne's] life, customs, and noble deeds, and to place before all men the image of a prince who was not fictitious, as was Xenophon's Cyrus, but truly by all nature endowed with many extraordinary gifts, and who appeared by divine will, so that he might serve as an example and a mirror of virtue for all the princes of the world to follow in their private and public rule" (quoted in Garin 1972, 88).

mirrors of princes that take him for their model, were it not for a pair of chapters found in the *Discourses*. In chapter 12 of book 2, Machiavelli considers whether it is better for a prince "to await the enemy inside his own borders or to go and meet him at home and assault him." He cites the advice Croesus gave to Cyrus to attack the Massageti in their own territory so as to deprive them of a place to fall back on and recover. Cyrus's acquiescence to this plan—in effect, trusting to the counsels of a former enemy[80]—led to the defeat of his army and his death at the hands of Queen Tomyris.[81] Machiavelli concludes the chapter with a general lesson. A prince whose subjects are unarmed and whose country is unaccustomed to war should always fight as far away from home as possible. But a prince like Cyrus, "whose people are armed and ordered for war, should await war at home and not go to encounter it."[82] Here the example of Cyrus, drawn entirely from the pages of Herodotus, is altogether negative. And when Machiavelli turns in the very next chapter to rehabilitate Cyrus, it is the Cyrus portrayed by Xenophon, not Herodotus.

Machiavelli devotes chapter 13 of book 2 of the *Discourses* to the subject "That One Comes from Base to Great Fortune More Through Fraud than Force." He cites some impressive examples taken from the *Cyropaedia*:

Xenophon in his life of Cyrus shows this necessity to deceive, considering that the first expedition that he has Cyrus make against the king of Armenia is full of fraud, and that he makes him seize his kingdom through deception and not through force. And he does not conclude otherwise from this action than that it is necessary for a prince who wishes to do great things to learn to deceive. Besides this, he makes him deceive Cyaxares, king of the Medes, his maternal uncle, in several modes; without which fraud he shows that Cyrus could not have attained the greatness he came to.[83]

This is a significant reconsideration of the appraisal Machiavelli offered in the *Prince*. There he seemed to reject the *Cyropaedia* as an imaginative work that naively counseled chastity, affability, human-

80. Cf. Machiavelli, *Prince*, 67.

81. Herodotus 1.205–15.

82. Machiavelli, *Discourses*, 2.12.1, 4. Letter to Francesco Vettori, 26 August 1513, Machiavelli 1983, 20: "[E]t troverrete coloro che hanno fatto gran fatti avere armati le populationi loro, come Nino gil Assiri, Ciro i Persi, Allessandro i Macedoni. . . ."

83. Machiavelli, *Discourses*, 2.13.1.

ity, and liberality as the keys to success and glory. Here he endorses the utility of Xenophon's account, even while stressing its fictional character.[84] The difference lies in the kind of advice that Machiavelli claims Xenophon offers. In the *Prince*, Xenophon represents "virtue"; in the *Discourses*, deceit, or what "the writers" would erroneously label "vice." Machiavelli objects then not to the imagination or fiction per se, but to the improper use of the imagination or fiction, that is, when they are employed to present a fallacious harmony between the demands of conventional morality and the necessities that govern politics. This leaves us with the following problem. Does the *Cyropaedia* recommend adherence to moral virtue, as the civic-humanists and the Machiavelli of the *Prince* seem to think? Or does it show the utility of fraud as a means to greatness (and not just the ordinarily excusable fraud practiced against enemies, but even and especially fraud deployed against a close relative and commander), as the Machiavelli of the *Discourses* maintains?[85] Did Machiavelli simply change his mind about the *Cyropaedia*, or, like Tatum and Gera, did he think Xenophon incoherently preached both views? Some help in resolving this paradox can be gained by returning to the *Prince*.

We have seen that in chapter 17 of the *Prince*, Machiavelli criticizes "the writers" for not having paid sufficient attention to the causes of political success—in particular, to the need for "inhuman cruelty" in a good general. But in chapter 18, he modifies this criticism, at least as regards "the ancient writers." According to Machiavelli, there are two kinds of combat: one with laws, proper to men; the other with force, proper to beasts. Combat with laws is often not enough, and so a prince must know well how to use both the beast (e.g., inhuman cruelty) and the man. But this is no new discovery. In fact, Machiavelli now claims it can be learned from certain writers, and, moreover, from the parts of their works often considered imaginary:

84. Ibid., "[Xenophon] has Cyrus make . . . he makes him seize . . . he makes him deceive." See Strauss 1984, 139.

85. Montaigne confirms the *Discourses'* reading of the *Cyropaedia*: "For it is not said that time and place serving, we should not make use of our enemies' foolishness, as we do of their cowardice. Indeed, war has many reasonable privileges to the prejudice of reason. And here the rule fails: 'No one should act to prey upon the ignorance of others.' But I am astonished at the scope that Xenophon gives these privileges, both by the discourse and various exploits of his perfect emperor. He is an author of marvelous weight in such matters and one of the first of Socrates's disciples" (*Essais*, 1.6).

This role was taught covertly to princes by ancient writers, who wrote that Achilles, and many other ancient princes, were given to Chiron the centaur to be raised, so that he would train them under his discipline. To have as a teacher a half-beast, half-man means nothing other than that a prince needs to know how to use one and the other nature; and the one without the other is not lasting.[86]

The real difficulty, at least with "the ancient writers," now appears to be not so much what they thought but how they wrote, and therefore how one reads them. Much like scholars such as Due, Scipio is so taken with the chastity, affability, humanity, and liberality present on the surface of Xenophon's portrait of Cyrus that he does not perceive those qualities that Cyrus must have had in common with a successful general like Hannibal (i.e., those to which Tatum and Gera are more reliable guides). For Machiavelli, the proof of Hannibal's inhuman cruelty was his ability to lead a very large army made up of different kinds of men through enemy territory without dissension, in bad as well as good fortune.[87] In the *Cyropaedia*, Cyrus accomplishes this same feat. Might Xenophon be one of those "ancient writers" whose books, according to Machiavelli, contain a covert teaching, one conveyed as much by the dramatic or mimetic character of the work as by any explicit utterances they contain? If so, then Scipio would seem to bear some measure of responsibility for the pernicious effect of the book. Careless and overly literal-minded readers like him are what make "imagined republics and principalities" so dangerous. Returning to the earlier passage from chapter 14 of the *Prince* with Machiavelli's strictures in mind, we can now see that his recommendation to read the *Cyropaedia* was as much an invitation to observe and reflect as to imitate and act. If we do so attentively, Machiavelli claims, we shall be able to recognize "how much [*quanto*] glory" Scipio's imitation of Cyrus brought him, and "how much" Scipio conformed to Cyrus's virtues. But in Machiavelli's usage, *quanto* can also mean "how little."[88] And if chapter 14 seems to link Cyrus and Scipio by virtue of their liberality, chapter 16 sets them at odds over the question of its proper use. Cyrus—and, following

    86. Machiavelli, *Prince*, 69.
    87. Ibid., 67.
    88. See, e.g., the first sentence of *The Prince*, ch. 18; *Discourses* 2.17.1 and 1.55.1 with 3.23. Tarcov 1982, 707.

him, a more discerning reader, Caesar—understood what the so-called savior of the Roman Republic failed to grasp.

And of what is not your own or your subjects', one can be a bigger giver as were Cyrus, Caesar, and Alexander, because spending what is someone else's does not take reputation away from you but adds it to you, only spending your own is what hurts you. And there is nothing that consumes itself as much as liberality.[89]

As Machiavelli makes explicit in the *Discourses*, it was Cyrus's use of fraud and not his other "virtues" that led to his greatness, much as it was the ability of the Roman Senate *to hide* Scipio's simple (*facile*) nature that made for his glory.[90] The difference between the presentation of Xenophon's Cyrus in the *Prince* and in the *Discourses* lies, not in Machiavelli's shifting judgment of his character, but in the greater candor of the latter work.

It is safe to assume that a reader of Machiavelli's acuity, to say nothing of his tastes, noted all of the disreputable practices that Tatum and Gera uncover in the *Cyropaedia*, and doubtless many others. But if he approves of and even imitates Cyrus's extensive use of fraud, he seems to have some reservations concerning the ultimate ends Cyrus pursued, as well as Xenophon's role in concealing those designs. These criticisms emerge in the course of Machiavelli's comparison of the contributions Manlius Torquatus and Valerius Corvinus made to the health and stability of republican Rome. Both were excellent captains, who achieved personal glory for their victories over Rome's enemies, but the manner in which they dealt with their soldiers differed markedly. Manlius commanded with severity, inflicting uninterrupted toil and punishments on his men. Valerius, on the other hand, proceeded humanely and according to a custom that was not hard to observe. When forced to deal with transgressors, he made sure they imputed the harshness of their punishments to the ordinances themselves and not to his personal cruelty. As Machiavelli explicitly notes, the two very much resembled Hannibal and Scipio, and they accordingly ran the risk of falling into their respective vices: for Hannibal and Manlius, arousing the soldiers' hatred; for Scipio and Valerius, their scorn.[91]

89. Machiavelli, *Prince*, 64.
90. Ibid., 68.
91. Machiavelli, *Discourses*, 3.22.1, 3.

If Manlius and Valerius won equal success against Rome's enemies, they do not earn Machiavelli's equal praise. He claims that Manlius's mode of proceeding was better for a republic. His harshness, love of the common good, and reverence for the fatherland—manifest in his ordering the execution of his own son—inspired his soldiers with obedience but did not win him "particular friends" or "partisans" who could then advance his (and their) "private ambitions." So useful was Manlius to Rome, Machiavelli claims, that "if a republic were so happy that it often had [such a] one who with his example might renew the laws, and not only restrain it from running to ruin but pull it back, it would be perpetual."[92] Machiavelli's judgment of Valerius is altogether different. His "kindness" and "humanity" earned him the goodwill of the soldiers, and this threatened to have "bad effects on freedom" when combined with the long military commands made inevitable by the expansion of the republic: "I conclude, therefore, that the proceeding of Valerius is useful in a prince and pernicious in a citizen, not only to the fatherland but to himself: to it, because those modes prepare the way to tyranny; to himself, because in suspecting his mode of proceeding, his city is constrained to secure itself against him to his harm."[93]

Machiavelli repeatedly and emphatically stresses the similarities between Valerius and Cyrus, or, rather, between Valerius and what "Xenophon writes" of Cyrus.[94] And what Xenophon writes of Cyrus is also calculated to appeal to the popular desire to be ruled by great men who are humane and beneficent in their affability, mercy, chastity, and liberality. In the *Cyropaedia*, Xenophon "toils very much to demonstrate how many [*quanti*] honors, how many victories, how much good fame being humane and affable brought to Cyrus, and not giving any example of himself either as proud, or as cruel, or as

---

92. Ibid., 3.22.3–4.
93. Ibid., 3.22.6.
94. Machiavelli, *Discourses*, 3.22.4–5: "Nonetheless, those who write about how a prince has to govern side more with Valerius than with Manlius; and Xenophon, cited before by me, by giving many examples of the humanity of Cyrus, *conforms very much* to what Titus Livy says of Valerius.... [For a prince] being an observer of the orders and being held virtuous give him obedience, affability, humanity, mercy, and the other parts that were in Valerius—*and that, Xenophon writes, were in Cyrus*—give him love" (emphasis added).

lustful, or as having any other vice that stains the life of men."[95] Even if Xenophon instructs his more astute readers as to the true foundation of political greatness, the enormous effort he expends to disguise the real causes of Cyrus's success, revealing them only to those who read with care and astuteness, serves to make it more difficult for a city to detect and secure itself against such a threat. For the many, like Scipio, will be taken in by the appealing surface. And in politics it is their beliefs that will ultimately have the final say.[96] Machiavelli's willingness to bring to light what Xenophon leaves in the shadows, be it Cyrus's extensive use of fraud or the secret of his renowned generosity, stands as a kind of rebuke to Xenophon's reticence. For, by exposing the true methods and motives of the great, Machiavelli puts his readers on guard against them,[97] even if in doing so he runs the "Manlian" and apparently self-sacrificing risk that his own name will forever become synonymous with harshness.[98] In effect, he accuses Xenophon of currying popular favor in a manner that aids and abets those who would indulge their tyrannical passions at the expense of republican freedom, of instructing potential Caesars at the expense of the less perceptive, if more decent, admirers of Scipio and his like. And if, as Machiavelli claims, the common good is observed only in republics, this too will surely suffer.[99]

Cyrus may well be Xenophon's model of a perfect prince. But we must always bear in mind that Cyrus begins his career as the duly elected general of a republic. The movement of the *Cyropaedia* as a whole follows his ascent to the office of universal monarch, and Machiavelli's analysis of the book reminds us that this is no less a transformation of citizens to subjects, republic to empire, freedom to despotism, virtue to corruption—in short, a movement one is hard-pressed simply to regard as progress. In this way, Machiavelli's treatment compels us once again to face the question raised, but left unresolved, by Gera, which also draws our attention to what makes the *Cyropaedia* almost unique in extant classical literature: what in Xenophon's understand-

95. Ibid., 3.20.1.
96. Machiavelli, *Prince*, 71.
97. See Rousseau, *Social Contract*, 3.6.
98. Machiavelli, *Discourses*, 3.22.1.
99. Ibid., 2.2.1.

ing of the classical republic could have led him to give an apparently laudatory presentation of its destruction?

Fundamental to my interpretive approach is the fact, stressed by Machiavelli and other early modern readers, that the *Cyropaedia* is neither a work of history nor a political treatise, but rather a drama. Edmund Spenser wrote most eloquently of this aspect of the book:

> For this cause is Xenophon preferred before Plato, for that the one in the exquisite depth of his judgment formed a common wealth such as it should be, but the other in the person of Cyrus and the Persians fashioned a government such as might best be. So much more profitable and gracious is doctrine by ensample than by rule.[100]

Reading the *Cyropaedia* therefore requires the kind of care one takes in interpreting a dialogue or play. Events must be evaluated in light of the contingencies faced by their actors, speeches must be checked against deeds and understood within their dramatic contexts, and the course or movement of the book as a whole must be taken into account. Above all, no single character, not even a prince, however perfect, can simply be assumed to express the author's views.

I have also found it useful to begin from the premise that Xenophon knew and paid attention to what he was doing when he wrote the *Cyropaedia*. If he did not conceive and execute the book in one coherent movement of his mind, it seems likely to me that he would have had the time and inclination to read through the manuscript at least once to make any necessary revisions or corrections before publication. There is certainly no external evidence to the contrary.[101] We should never rule out the possibility of authorial incompetence or corruptions of transmission, but these seem to me explanations of last resort. My own experience in reading Xenophon, which I have tried to reproduce in some measure for the reader of this study, has been one of continuous discovery and amazement at the wealth of interlocking details that make up his compositions. If, as Xenophon's Socrates observes, the presence of design in the world makes plausible the inference of an intelligent creator, might not the same hold true for a work of literature?[102] True, this approach runs the risk of taking as

100. Spenser, *Faerie Queene*, 75. Cf. Sidney, *Defense of Poesy*, 103, 108, 109–10.
101. Cf. Tuplin 1993, 167.
102. *Mem.* 1.4.

a given something I hope in part to demonstrate: namely, the unity and coherence of Xenophon's thought. But this is an ill from which the opposite procedure is no more immune, and the only remedy for which is to keep the danger always in mind. Such a beginning point is also what I take to be the more natural and generous assumption with any author. In the particular case of Xenophon, it is one made all the more plausible by the admiration and praise of readers of otherwise unimpeachable intellectual stature. The proof of the pudding, however, remains as always in the eating.[103]

103. Cf. the epigraph from Montaigne, vii.

Chapter One

Republic

Xenophon's Opening Reflections

Xenophon begins the *Cyropaedia* with a general reflection on political instability and its causes. Democracies are overthrown by those who wish to live under any other form of government; monarchies and oligarchies are abolished by the people. Tyrannies are particularly unstable, although those who manage to establish them, even if for just a short period of time, are wondered at as being wise and fortunate. The situation is altogether different with the kind of rule exercised by human beings over certain kinds of animals. Herds that resist strangers (ἀλλόφυλοι) follow and obey their rulers and allow them to enjoy whatever profit accrues. They never conspire against their keepers, whereas human beings do so against no one sooner than those they perceive attempting to rule over them. The problem seems to be that it is better to rule than to be ruled, to profit than to be profited from. (Hence the belief that tyrants, who represent the extreme of advantageous rule, are wise and fortunate.) Man, being so constituted by nature as to be aware of this fact, thus turns out to be the most difficult of animals to rule. Xenophon seems ready to accept this general conclusion, were it not for the example of Cyrus, the Persian. His ability to secure the obedience of a vast number of men, cities, and nations "compelled us to change our opinion and to conclude that ruling human beings is neither impossible nor difficult provided someone does it with knowledge" (ἐπισταμένως, 1.1.1–3).

Cyrus attracts Xenophon's attention first of all as one who appears to have solved the difficult problem of ruling human beings, who perhaps possesses the art or science of rule spoken of by Socrates.[1] This starting point would account for what many have taken to be a chief peculiarity of the *Cyropaedia*, namely, that an Athenian should offer as his model of a "perfect king" the barbarian founder of an empire that would eventually come to invade, occupy, and nearly destroy his native city. Yet the universalism inherent in the idea of a technical art or science necessarily transcends accidental distinctions of time and place or nationality. From such a perspective, the fact that Cyrus is a Persian, or that he lived in the distant past, is of little or no importance. Indeed, this willingness to look beyond the narrow limits of his own time and culture for guidance in matters of the greatest importance is what marks Xenophon as a true "Greek." Like Plato, he sees no reason why the best regime or ruler might not come into existence "in some barbarian place, well beyond our sight,"[2] Yet we shall be disappointed in our expectation if we then think the *Cyropaedia* will take the form of a technical treatise or meditation on some nameless ideal, such as Plato presents in his *Statesman*. The "proof" that Xenophon relies on to show that Cyrus ruled "with knowledge" is the fact of his great historical success. But quite apart from a certain exaggeration of its geographical extent (1.1.4; 8.8.1),[3] Cyrus himself admits that success can often fall to those who are altogether ignorant (7.5.76; cf. *CL* 1.1). Nor does knowledge by any means guarantee a favorable outcome (1.6.23, 46; 3.1.38).

At the close of the opening chapter, Xenophon instead sets himself the task of explaining Cyrus's phenomenal success through an investigation of his birth (γενεά), nature (φύσις), and education (παιδεία): factors that would seem to have no intrinsic connection with the possession or practice of the science of rule. The *Cyropaedia* then resembles nothing so much as a biography,[4] from which one would as little expect to learn a science as to master modern physics from an account of the

---

1. "[Socrates] said that kings and rulers are not those who hold the scepters, nor those elected by any chance persons, nor those who obtain office by lot, nor those who have used violence, nor those who have used deceit, but those who know how to rule [ἐπιστάμενοι ἄρχειν, *Mem.* 3.9.10]."

2. Plato *Republic* 499c–d; cf. 470c–e. By the very fact of having written the *Cyropaedia*, Xenophon distinguishes himself from the typical or conventional Greek, for instance, from Agesilaus (*Ages.* 7.4–7).

3. For Xenophon's view of the importance of size or extent, see *Hel.* 7.2.1.

4. Momigliano 1991, 55: "The *Cyropaedia* is indeed the most accomplished biography we have in classical Greek literature."

life and times of Albert Einstein. Yet, even as biography, it falls far
short of delivering the facts of Cyrus's life. Xenophon, as we have
already noted, is not particularly interested in the "historical truth."
If the *Cyropaedia* is an essentially fictional account, however, it remains somewhat puzzling why Xenophon chose to base his narrative,
however loosely, on the historical character of a Persian king. Yet the
figure of Cyrus seems to have held considerable attraction for some
of Xenophon's contemporaries.[5] Seeking to convince a wealthy young
Athenian of the dignity of agriculture, Socrates can do no better, for
example, than to associate farming with Cyrus, "a king of a very high
reputation."[6] And Ischomachus, the perfect Athenian gentleman, takes
the laws of the Persian king as models for the just management of his
household. Perhaps the most striking testimony is related by Plato. His
Socrates observes of the young Alcibiades, whose guardian, Pericles,
was one of Athens's greatest statesmen, "I suppose that you believe,
apart from Cyrus and Xerxes, no one worthy of mention has ever
existed."[7] The common thread that links these Greek admirers of the
Persian king is not so much the desire for knowledge of the science
of rule as, first and foremost, a desire to distinguish themselves by
nobility. And, like the desire for knowledge, this passion can have a
kind of broadening effect; in aiming at certain forms of human excellence, it, too, contains the potential to transcend narrow political
or ethnic categories. The sheer size and grandeur of the Persian empire, its wealth and power, command the respect of those who share
its aims and ambitions, even when they find themselves oppressed
or threatened by it. Xenophon's choice of Cyrus would, then, seem
calculated to appeal to the passions of a class of men who seem to have
interested his own teacher, Socrates, so much—namely, "those longing
for the noble things," among which political rule is almost always given
a prominent place.[8]

If Xenophon appeals to the prejudices of such readers, he does not
indulge them. Matters that might be thought to interest them most are
covered with astonishing brevity. Concerning Cyrus's birth, Xenophon

5. The Socratic Antisthenes is reported to have written a *Cyrus*. See Giannantoni
1985, 189–201, 269–81, for a discussion of the remaining fragments.
6. *Oec.* 4.4, 4.16–17.
7. Plato *Alcibiades I* 105c.
8. *Mem.* 3.1.1.

relates only that his father "is said to be" Cambyses, king of the Persians and a descendant of the hero Perseus. His mother, "it is agreed," was Mandane, daughter of the Median king Astyages. As for his nature, "it is said and sung even now among the barbarians that he was in form most beautiful, in soul most benevolent"(φιλανθρωπότατος), the greatest lover of learning and the most ambitious (φιλοτιμότατος, 1.2.1).[9] Xenophon's own interest, if we take the title of the book to give some indication, is primarily in the education Cyrus received. And that education reflects little of the imperial splendor that so captivates Cyrus's Athenian admirers. According to Xenophon's conceit, Cyrus received his first formation under the laws governing a small and isolated polis. To grasp the character and aims of that education, one must understand the regime of which it forms a part.[10] The description of Cyrus's earliest education is at the same time Xenophon's analysis of the classical republican regime.

Persian Education

Xenophon's Persia is an unusual if not singular place. Whereas in most cities parents are allowed to educate their children as they wish, while the elderly live as they please, and the laws command the citizens not to steal, rob, break into houses, beat those they have no right to, commit adultery, or disobey the rulers, in Persia the laws start from a different point in the care they take to secure the common good. They look to provide an early and extremely public education, so that "from the beginning the citizens shall not be such as to desire [to commit] any bad or shameful deed" (1.2.3). To this end, the Persians have a "so-called Free Square" where all buying and selling, as well as those practicing the banausic arts, are forbidden, lest their vulgarity and tumults disturb the orderliness of those who have been or are being educated. This square is divided into four parts, which correspond to the different ages and duties of the citizens: boys, youths, mature men,

9. Xenophon frequently uses λέγεται, "it is said," to relate information that he considers doubtful or necessarily uncertain and which he often later modifies or rejects. In this instance, consider what Xenophon later says in his own name of Cyrus's qualities at 1.3.3, 1.4.1, 3. See also *Hel.* 3.3.2 with *Ages.* 1.5.

10. *Mem.* 1.2.40–46; *Poroi* 1.1; *Cyro.* 1.2.15; *CL* 4.1–2. For the interrelation of education (παιδεία) and regime (πολιτεία), see Rahe 1994, 10–13.

and elders. The boys and men are required to come each day at dawn; the youths must also pass their nights there; the elders arrive at their convenience, except on certain appointed days, when their presence is obligatory. Within these four groups, the Persians are divided into twelve tribes, which compete against one another in various contests.

The young boys are constantly in the charge of certain elders elected to rule over them. They attend schools of justice and are trained to be moderate, self-controlled, and obedient to their rulers. At the age of sixteen or seventeen, they enter the ranks of youths, where they continue their earlier training and also learn the skills of the hunt. If the youths fulfill their duties without reproach for ten years, they become members of the class of mature men. Like the youths, these men are at the disposal of the rulers to serve the community (τὸ κοινόν), especially in matters demanding prudence and bodily strength. Whenever there is a military expedition, they put aside the weapons of the hunt and take up those used for fighting at close quarters. All of the officers, with the exception of the teachers of the boys and judges, are selected from this class. After twenty-five years of dutiful military service, these men pass into the ranks of the elders and are no longer required to go to war outside their country. Instead, they remain at home and try cases of law, in particular, those involving a capital offense. They also elect all of the officers and sit in judgment on the youths and men accused of neglecting their duties (1.2.5–6, 9–10, 13–14).

Even this brief sketch is sufficient to show that Xenophon's Persia bears no resemblance to what little is known of the historical Persia.[11] As frequently noted, the Persia he describes at the beginning of the *Cyropaedia* bears many similarities to the Sparta of his *Constitution of the Lacedaemonians*.[12] Both Sparta and Xenophon's Persia are republics, with kings whose powers are limited to religious and military matters and subject to the control of a council of elders; both make education an entirely public concern and look down on money-making and the manual arts. The Persian kings claim descent from the hero Perseus, as Sparta's do from Heracles. Xenophon's Persians worship

11. Gibbon 1994, 3: 381, "According to the first book of the *Cyropaedia*, professors of tactics, a small part of the science of war, were already instituted in Persia, by which Greece must be understood."
12. Delebecque 1957, 385; Grant 1872, 126–128; Croiset 1873, 147, 150; Carlier 1978, 138–41; Gera 1993, 76, 155–56; Tuplin 1994, 134–161.

and swear by Greek gods and heroes and sing a paean on going into battle. Xenophon even uses distinctively Spartan technical terms to describe the Persians; the Spartan ruling class call themselves the ὅμοιοι, the Persian equivalent, ὁμότιμοι; among both, a fundamental law is called a ῥήτρα; and Xenophon's Persians are even said to use a special kind of Lacedaemonian cup designed for drinking from muddy water, a κώθων.

Scholars who take Xenophon to be a whole-hearted laconophile find nothing surprising in these parallels and believe the *Cyropaedia* to be yet another manifestation of his pro-Spartan enthusiasm,[13] a bias that they reduce to an expression of his allegedly oligarchic class prejudices, his bitterness at being exiled from democratic Athens, and the wish to flatter a city that had perhaps rewarded some service with a grant of land in Scillus.[14] Yet those who hold these views overlook the fact that Xenophon can be as critical of oligarchy as of democracy, that nowhere in his writings is there the least trace of bitterness or rancor over his exile, and that he considered it an error of the vulgar to confuse the good man (or city) with one's benefactor.[15] But even if the extent of Xenophon's pro-Spartan sympathies has been exaggerated, do not the similarities between his Persia and the Spartan regime call into question his reliability as a historian and demonstrate his inability to think outside the narrow conventions of Greek political categories? Pericles Georges, for example, claims that the resemblance between Sparta and the Persia of the *Cyropaedia* is a manifestation of Xenophon's unconscious prejudices: if the Persians under Cyrus were successful, they must have been virtuous and good; and if virtuous and good, then to Xenophon's mind they must have been like Spartan Greeks.[16] This objection, however, misunderstands the fundamentally theoretical (and not historical) intention of the work. Xenophon, like Thucydides, recognized that the Greeks had once been barbarians, and that what made for their singular way of life was somehow connected with Sparta's discovery or invention

13. Prinz, 1911 goes so far as to read the *Cyropaedia* as a programmatic *roman à clef* with Cyrus representing the Spartan general Agesilaus. See Scharr 1919 for a rejoinder.
14. E.g., Luccioni 1949, 9, 32, 36 n. 34, 162.
15. *Mem.* 1.2.43; *Hel.* 7.3.12; *Cyro.* 3.3.4.
16. Georges 1994, 229.

of "the common." There, in an attempt to overcome endemic civil strife, the rich assimilated to the ways of the *demos* and stripped themselves of conventional distinctions, competing naked in public— man against man and on the basis of equality—in order to establish the rule of natural superiority.[17] The *Cyropaedia* is not about the Persia that Xenophon or any of his putative sources knew at first- or secondhand, but rather the "Persia" that Greece could and would once again become with the destruction of the political way of life embodied by the polis. For this reason, what Christopher Tuplin has dubbed the "Persian decor" of the *Cyropaedia* is present more at the end than at the beginning of the book.[18] Nor need we look for an explanation of the Spartan character of the initial Persian republic in the necessarily ambiguous circumstances of Xenophon's biography, for example, in his alleged gratitude or groveling for a grant of land, which Sparta may or may not have bestowed on him.[19] A keen interest in Sparta was, after all, shared by Herodotus, Thucydides, Plato, Aristotle, and virtually every political philosopher and historian in the classical world, to say nothing of the fascination Sparta excited among European thinkers from the Renaissance up to the end of the eighteenth century.[20] Sparta has in all times and places represented the incarnation of the spirit of republican politics. Paul Rahe explains, "She did this by taking the institutions and practices embryonic in every *polis* and

17. Thucydides 1.6.3–5. Orwin 1994, 31; Forde 1989, 53.

18. Tuplin 1990 and 1994. Tuplin's otherwise thorough comparison of Sparta and Persia is marred by his occasional failure to make the necessary distinction between the two "Persias" presented in the *Cyropaedia*, the republic of the beginning and the empire established at the end. For example, he denies that Xenophon's Persia suffers from the oliganthropy so notable in Sparta. This is true of the Persian empire, but the small number of full citizens or peers is an important and constitutive element of the original republic. See, e.g., 2.1.3.

19. See Niebuhr 1828, 1: 464ff., for an early and influential attack on Xenophon for having fought with Sparta and her allies against Athens. The historical example of Critias may prove that it was possible to be an Athenian and a passionate laconophile, a sometime associate of Socrates, an exile, and the author of a work entitled the *Constitution of the Lacedaemonians*. But his precedent is in no way binding on Xenophon, who explicitly censors Critias in the *Memorabilia*. In antiquity, Xenophon was noted for his impartiality (Lucian, *How to Write History* 39). This assessment is undergoing a revival. For Xenophon's even-handed criticisms of both Sparta and Athens in the *Hellenica*, see Tuplin 1989, esp. 163–68.

20. Rawson 1969.

developing them into an extreme only imagined elsewhere."[21] But if Xenophon takes Sparta to be the epitome of Greek political life, it is not a model to which he slavishly adheres. As Arnaldo Momigliano notes, Xenophon's Persia is *un ideale lontanissimo da Sparta.*[22] But to present an idealized portrait, especially a very distant one, means to be aware of faults and defects in the original, and therefore to be something less than its wholehearted partisan. In order to see what improvements Xenophon introduces into his Persian republic, we must first understand in what way he thought the Spartan regime fell short.

The composition of the *Constitution of the Lacedaemonians* finds its origins in Xenophon's wonder both at Sparta, which, despite her small population, became the most powerful city in Greece, and at Lycurgus, who established her laws (*CL*, 1.1–2). Lycurgus's legislation was distinctive in that it "compelled all those in Sparta to practice all the virtues"; or, as Xenophon elaborates, "he established it as an irresistible necessity to practice the whole of political virtue" (10.4, 7). The qualities that Xenophon identifies among the Spartans, and at which they excelled, are continence, shame, obedience, and courage (2.14, 9ff., 4.2). Continence (ἐγκράτεια) is the virtue that controls the pleasures of the body and those involving the use of wealth.[23] To habituate them to endure the extremes of heat and cold, Spartan boys went without shoes and wore but one garment throughout the year. Their food was strictly regulated in the name of health and to develop in them the ability to toil on an empty stomach. This diet left the children in a constant state of hunger, which Lycurgus allowed them to alleviate by stealing food. He did this not out of a concern for their suffering or nutrition, but as a means of making them more cunning and warlike. Those who "stole badly"—that is, those who were caught—were severely beaten. Thus, according to Xenophon, Spartan legislation concerning continence was based on the unspoken

21. Rahe 1994, 125, 147.

22. Momigliano 1966, 345. Carlier 1978, 142: "La παιδεία de la *Cyropédie* est plus qu'une imitation de Sparte: c'est la projection dans un lointain passé perse de conceptions, d'idéaux et de projets de reforme assez répandus dans toute la Grèce vers 360." Cf. Tuplin 1994, 139.

23. *Mem.* 1.5.6.

premise, made explicit elsewhere in his writings,[24] that undetected theft is honorable and good (2.4–8; cf. 10.5–6, and ἦν at 6.2).

Lycurgus also forbade the Spartans to practice any money-making arts, allowed them to make use of one another's property as if it were held in common, and insisted on equality in the sharing of food and other supplies (6.3–4; 7.1–3). His method of eliminating the desire for wealth from the souls of his citizens was to make its possession all but useless. In this spirit, he made the coinage large and cumbersome, so that it was almost worthless outside the community and more difficult to hide within it (7.5). Nevertheless, Xenophon indicates that these measures did not attain their end. Distinctions between rich and poor remained politically important, and searches were undertaken to look for hidden gold and silver (5.3; 6.5; 7.6; 10.7; 13.11). Xenophon makes clear the nature of the problem Lycurgus faced when he remarks, "I know in former times they feared *to be seen* in the possession of gold" (13.3; emphasis added). This difficulty was of course exacerbated by the instruction the citizens received to make them expert in various covert activities.

Shame, the passion or sentiment that prevents us, not so much from committing indecent acts, as from appearing to do so, proved to be the true foundation of the Spartans' virtues.[25] Lycurgus inculcated it in the young through punishment and perpetual (ἀεί) surveillance (2.2, 10; 3.4). Among the mature and elderly, its effects were enhanced by the widespread use of spies and the extremely public nature of their way of life (1.5; 2.13; 3.5; 4.4; 5.5). Obedience to the laws and magistrates, which the Spartans held to be "the greatest good," was similarly enforced by beatings and the impositions of fines. The result was a herdlike mentality that caused Spartans to follow wherever they were led (2.2; 4.6; 8.1–3). What "willing obedience" the Spartans did render was obtained by the use of various cunning devices (μηχανημάτων), such as promulgating the belief that their laws had been given to them by the god Apollo, an opinion that Xenophon considered false (8.5).

How, then, did Sparta not only preserve itself but even triumph over Athens, an enlightened imperial power? The answer lies in the citizens' singular devotion to the arts of war and the cultivation of courage or

24. *Anab.* 4.6.14–15.
25. Cf. *Mem.* 1.5.4.

manliness (9ff., 12.7).[26] While the particular brutality of Helot slavery, especially when combined with the small number of Spartans, no doubt contributed to their meticulous attention to such matters (1.4; 12.2–4; 6.3; 1.1), the exact identification Lycurgus managed to establish in citizens' souls between the wicked man and the coward was more important. He "contrived" (ἐμηχανήσατο) that the life of such a man be so wretched that even death was preferable (10.6; 8.3; 11.4–6).[27] Yet, in Xenophon's opinion, courage by itself is indistinguishable from a dangerous lack of sense.[28] He indicates his judgment of the superficial or sham character of the Spartans' "virtues" by his failure to attribute the real virtues of justice and moderation (σωφροσύνη) to them.[29] The absence of moderation is all the more striking given its importance in Critias's *Constitution of the Lacedaemonians*, the work Xenophon imitates and parodies in his own;[30] and justice figures quite prominently in Xenophon's improved "Persian" ideal.[31]

Whereas the bulk of the *Cyropaedia* is written in the past tense, Xenophon's account of the Persian regime and education is related in the present, setting it off from the rest of the work and imparting to it an air of timelessness.[32] Its relation to the historical Sparta is similar to that of the regime found in Plato's *Republic*.[33] What Xenophon does is to purge the Spartan regime of the unnecessary extremism and faults that he identifies in the *Constitution of the Lacedaemonians*. He presents the republican regime in its best possible form. Here the Persian boys are "taught" both continence and moderation in a manner undocumented among the Spartans; they actually see their elders practicing them and thus learn by example.[34] Continence with

26. Cf. Aristotle *Politics* 1271b.

27. Cf. *Hel.* 4.5.11–19. For striking examples, see Herodotus 7.229–31, 9.71, and 1.82.

28. *Ages.* 2.12, 6.1, 2.7; *Hel.* 4.3.19.

29. *Mem.* 3.9.4 with *CL* 1.2. τὸ σωφρονεῖν at *CL* 3.4 is grammatically ambiguous and, in light of 3.5, no doubt ironic; 14.5 should be considered with *Cyro.* 8.1.31.

30. See Critias fr. 6 in Diels 1903, 379.

31. For a fuller analysis of Xenophon's *Constitution of the Lacedaemonians*, see Strauss 1939, Momigliano 1966, and Proietti 1987, all of which I have drawn on here.

32. Newell 1981, 24.

33. See Aulus Gellius, *Attic Nights* 14.3.

34. The verb "to teach"(διδάσκειν) and its related noun "school"(διδασκαλεῖον) occur in the *Constitution of the Lacedaemonians* only with reference to non-Spartan practices. See Montaigne, *Essais*, 1.25.

regard to food and drink is also encouraged by the very plain fare of the
Persians; and the boys eat with their teachers, not at home, lest their
mothers overindulge them (1.2.8; *CL* 2.1).[35] Hunger may from time to
time provide the sauce for a meal (1.2.11; 1.5.1, 12), but it does not play
the central role it did in Spartan pedagogy. Accordingly, stealing food
is neither taught nor encouraged. Military skills and endurance of heat
and cold are developed on frequent hunting expeditions, paid for out
of the public treasury (1.2.10). When the boys graduate to the ranks of
the youths, they also start to spend their nights camped out around
the public buildings "for the sake of guarding the city and [practicing]
moderation" (1.2.9).

While the Spartans compel civic virtue by withholding food and
administering frequent beatings, the Persians make more use of praise
and blame (1.2.12). "Teaching" by means of the stomach may be
appropriate for taming wild beasts, but the use of speech (λόγος)
and the appeal to love of honor (φιλοτιμία) are more proper means
for the instruction of human beings.[36] While neither the Spartans nor
Persians give their children an education in letters, the distinctively
human capacity for speech finds some encouragement in the Persian
schools of justice, if only incidentally (1.4.3).[37] The replacement of the
Spartan emphasis on courage with this stress on justice is the most
impressive and far-reaching reform that Xenophon introduces into the

35. Cf. Plato *Laws* 694a–696a.

36. "Other living things, Socrates, learn to obey in these two ways: by being
punished when they try to disobey, and by being well treated when they serve eagerly.
Colts, at any rate, learn to obey the colt breakers by getting something that is pleasant
to them when they obey and getting into trouble when they disobey, until they become
subservient to the mind of the colt breaker; and puppies, though they are far inferior
to human beings in both mind and tongue, nevertheless learn in some way to run
in a circle and turn somersaults and many other things. For when they obey, they
get something they need, and when they are negligent, they are punished. As for
human beings, it's possible to make them more obedient in addition by speech, by
displaying to them how advantageous it is for them to obey; and yet for slaves the
education that seems fit only for beasts is effective also in teaching them to obey, for in
gratifying their bellies to the extent they desire, you can accomplish much with them.
But the ambitious natures are hungry for praise as others are for food and drink"
(*Oec.* 13.9).

37. *On Horsemanship* 8.13: "Whereas the gods have given to men to teach one
another by speech (λόγῳ) what they must do, it is clear that you can teach a horse
nothing by speech." Cf. *Mem.* 3.3.11.

Persian republic.[38] The children's instruction is facilitated by the fact that among them, as with grown men, there occur various disputes and conflicts. The rulers make the best of this and turn each transgression into an occasion to impress upon their minds the dictates of justice. One can estimate the frequency of such disputes by the fact that they spend "most of the day" sitting in judgment, while the children listen. They punish those guilty of the usual crimes, as well as those who make false accusations. In addition, "they bring one another to trial charged with the offence for which people hate one another the most, but go to trial least: ingratitude. Those found guilty are punished severely." This unusual practice reflects the Persians' seriousness about justice or devotion to the common good. For when gratitude regularly follows from such services, they are more likely to be forthcoming, and the tension between self-sacrifice and self-interest diminished (cf. 8.3.49). But the Persians also punish ingratitude because they think "it leads to all the shameful things," such as neglect of the gods, parents, fatherland, and friends—the sources of the greatest benefits and hence the objects of our deepest loyalties.

Unlike the Spartans, the Persians do not believe or teach that their laws were given by the gods.[39] Piety goes unmentioned in Xenophon's description of the ideal republican regime, but we learn from a later conversation, in which Cyrus recounts the lessons of his youth, that the Persians believe that in order to keep the gods gracious and willing to give counsel one should remember them in times of prosperity, rather than fawning on them only when in distress. Gods and friends should be cared for in the same way (1.6.3). But Persian piety is not simply mercenary.[40] Sacrificing to the gods in good times so that they will come to their aid in bad times exhausts the Persians' religious obligations as little as pacts of mutual defense exhaust the duties of friendship among men. The Persians also believe that only those who have made themselves such as they ought to be should ask for good things from the gods. And what they ought to be is hardworking, careful, and attentive students of those things the gods have given

38. Justice is among the first subjects taken up by Socrates in his instruction of Euthydemus, an exchange that serves as a kind of model for others (*Mem.* 4.2.11–23).

39. Cf. *CL* 8.5.

40. Cf. Farber 1979, 501. Farber's characterization is more accurately applied to Cyrus's "mature" view, not the Persians'. See 8.1.25.

them to learn. It is therefore not right (οὐδὲ θέμις) for someone who
has not learned to ride to ask the gods for victory in a cavalry battle,
or for someone who does not know how to shoot or to steer to ask
to excel at marksmanship or to rescue a ship at sea. Likewise, it is
impious for a farmer who has not planted to pray for a fine crop,
or for those who are reckless to pray for safety in war. "All these
things are contrary to the ordinances (θεσμοί) of the gods" (1.6.3–
6). The Persians hold the politically salutary opinion that the gods
help those who help themselves.[41] Yet considering human life, with
its endless toils and hardships, the scarcity of goods, and the uniquely
human dependence on the arts, one might perhaps come to doubt the
benevolence of the gods, to question their friendship, even to reproach
them for the way the world is ordered.[42] Indeed, human beings find
it difficult to reconcile the necessity of practicing the arts with divine
beneficence unless they believe, as the Persians do, that the arts have
been revealed to them by the gods (1.6.5ff., cf. 7.5.79). In this way, the
Persians understand their dependence on the gods to be compatible
with, and even to encourage, a large degree of human initiative. For
someone who makes himself such as he ought to be, learns what the
gods have given to learn, and then prays, a successful outcome is likely,
if not certain, especially if he has been careful to gain the friendship of
the gods by earlier sacrifices (cf. 1.5.14).

The principal means by which the Persians make themselves such as
they ought to be—that is to say, "the best"—is their regime (πολιτεία,
1.2.15; 1.2.1). This confidence in the superiority of the Persian way
of life makes intelligible the importance that they, like the Spartans,
place on obedience to the magistrates and laws. Only in the best
regime does the identity of the good man coincide with that of the
dutiful citizen and the virtue of obedience lose its usual ambiguity.[43]
Yet if the Persians are convinced of the superiority of their regime,
certain peculiarities in Xenophon's manner of presenting their claims
raise doubts as to whether he shared their opinion. He first indicates his

41. Carlier 1978, 141: "[D]'après Xénophon, les dieux n'accordent leur appui
qu'à ceux qui ont déjà pris eux mêmes toutes les mesures à leur portée en vue du
succès. Les conseils que donne Cambyse à Cyrus évoquent la maxime 'Aide-toi, le
ciel t'aidera.'"
42. Cf. *Oec.* 8.11–16; *Mem.* 1.3.12, 1.4.12–14, 2.3.19; *Cyro.* 7.1.11.
43. Aristotle *Politics* 1277b33–1278b5.

reservations when relating how the Persians select their magistrates. To have charge of the boys, they choose those among the elders "who seem likely to produce the best boys," and of the youths, those of the mature men "who seem likely to make them the best youths." We expect Xenophon to relate that they choose as rulers over the mature men those who likewise make them the best. But he breaks the pattern he has established and tells us instead that they choose "those who seem most likely to make them the best executors of the orders and requirements of the highest authority" (1.2.5). The full citizens are never said to be simply the best men. Apparently, they fail to live up to their formal appellation as "complete" or "perfect men" (τέλεοι ἄνδρες). Xenophon confirms this when he describes "the elders," and only the elders, as "those who are such as they are also called"(ὄντας τε καὶ καλουμένους).[44]

Xenophon's most incisive statement in the chapter devoted to the structure and working of the republican regime concerns the economic conditions in Persia and their bearing on the system of education. Xenophon marks this new phase in his analysis and signals his break with the communal spirit of Persia when he writes for the first time in the first person singular: "In order that the Persian regime come to light more clearly in its entirety [πᾶσα ἡ Περσῶν πολιτεία], I shall go back a little; for from what has already been said it may now be made clear in very few words." Xenophon goes on to relate that of the 120,000 Persian men, not one is excluded by law from attaining honor or public office.[45] All alike are permitted to attend the common schools of justice, where advancement through the ranks is based on merit. On the face of it, Xenophon's Persian republic is then an aristocracy, although a democratic one, since it establishes equality before the law as a central principle. But in practice this equality turns out to be limited by the extreme poverty of life in Persia. Only those in a

44. Bruell 1969, 12 n. 1.
45. Xenophon's figure of 120,000 for the total population of Persians has caused considerable embarrassment and debate among those who look to the *Cyropaedia* for historical information about Persia. The actual number of Persians at the time is thought to have been around 1,000,000. The most common explanation of this discrepancy is to assume that Xenophon counts only the peers (Miller 1983, 23). This approach is difficult to reconcile with the fact that even in the face of a serious foreign threat, no more than 1,000 peers are ever enlisted in the effort to defeat it.

position to maintain their children without putting them to work can send them to school; and only those who complete the training given to the boys can pass into the ranks of the youths, and so on (1.2.15). Children whose families lack the wherewithal to keep them in school can never become members of the class of "peers" (the ὁμότιμοι) and are effectively barred from public honors and office. But without doubt there are some born into poor families who have the natural capacity to make better use of the education than at least some of those born into wealth. The case of Pheraulus, a commoner who quickly rises to a place of great responsibility and rank once these barriers are removed, is perhaps only the most extreme example of the talents left uncultivated by the original Persian regime (8.3.2 ff.).

With his habitual reticence and delicacy, Xenophon leaves his readers to think through for themselves the implications that follow, "to go back a little" and reconsider his earlier description in the light cast by this disclosure. The peers are barred from any productive or mercantile occupation and pass almost all of their time hunting or attending to public affairs. This forces us to raise the indelicate question of how they support themselves. There is only one way.[46] A democratic aristocracy in principle, a hereditary oligarchy in practice, Persia is in fact ruled by men who owe their positions less to merit than to the possession of the arms and training that allow them to live off the labor of the "uneducated."[47] The resulting tension between the two classes, commoners and peers, determines much of the character of the regime. Forced to camp out every night around the public buildings in order to guard the city, not least of all from internal threats, the Persians make a virtue of this necessity and call it "moderation."[48] Xenophon never gives an exact account of the number of peers and commoners, but an estimate of their proportion

46. *Hipparchicus* 8.8: "Men must either work or eat from the work of others."

47. Cf. 2.1.3. Cambyses' observation at 1.6.17—"The hardest [burden] of all is to support an idle army. For not only are the eaters in an army many, but the supplies they draw on are limited. . . ."—should be applied to the domestic situation in Persia. Cf. *CL* 1.4, 6.1–3; *Poroi* 1.1 with 4.17–31.

48. Consider the implications of ἔξω at 1.2.14. Xenophon's insight also explains the remarkable absence of the terms ὁμόνοια and εὐνομία from his description of the Persian polis and almost from the *Cyropaedia* altogether. Cyrus will later consider ὁμόνοια to be something a ruler must be on guard against in his subjects (5.5.11; cf. *Mem.* 4.4.16, 4.6.14–15).

can be made on the basis of information he gives elsewhere. There are altogether 120,000 Persians. The force Cyrus leads out of Persia is made up of 1,000 peers and 30,000 commoners. Later, reinforcements of 40,000 commoners are sent out and Cyrus eventually takes another 10,000 commoners for his bodyguard (1.2.15; 1.5.5; 5.5.3; 7.5.68). As in Sparta, there are relatively few full Persian citizens.[49] The small number accounts for their assiduous devotion to physical exercises and hunting, which in turn form the basis of their military skills and discipline (1.2.10).[50] These skills are further developed by the many martial contests in which the peers constantly compete and that determine the distribution of honors (1.2.12).[51] The praise accorded success in these contests is the only personal goal encouraged among the Persians. For honors given to reward what is ultimately of service to the city create a common ground between individual and community interests, satisfying to some degree the desire for individual fulfillment, while binding that individual to those who hold him in esteem (1.2.9). Yet praise bestowed on all ceases to be praise, and the sweetest honors are those one tastes alone. The spirit of competition and the desire for distinction, such effective goads to excellence, also encourage and even create faction and enmity, especially where it is possible to advance as much by another's faults as one's own merits (1.2.14; 3.3.10; 6.2.4).[52] This accounts for the Persians' special concern with punishing false accusations (1.2.7). But if such strife is held in check by their instruction in justice and the strong conviction of the superiority of their own way of life, its worst excesses are also contained by a healthy fear of its political consequences, a fear made more acute by the presence of so many disenfranchised commoners (1.2.5, 15; 1.5.1).

What makes the republican regime distinctive and of particular interest to Xenophon is its claim to establish the common good by making its citizens "the best," that is, men who are simply good and

49. 2.1.3. In Herodotus's time, the ratio of Helots to Spartans was about 7:1. By Xenophon's time the proportion was likely even more extreme. See Rahe 1994, 127.

50. Hirsch 1985, 87, and Tuplin 1994, 140, stress the extent to which the Persian education, unlike the Spartan, is not militaristic. It would be more precise to say that its military character is better concealed.

51. Cf. *CL*, 4.5.

52. Cf. *Mem.* 2.6.17–20.

who practice virtue for its own sake (1.5.8–9). Its foundation is a public
education in justice that aims to cultivate wholehearted obedience to
the laws, which are, in turn, understood by the citizens to constitute the
best regime. Such an education includes a lengthy period of training
to break the citizens of the more selfish passions and interests, which
seem to grow in human beings without instruction or compulsion
(1.6.32). Austerity is its appropriate accompaniment, removing as it
does the objects of so many private pleasures and habituating the
citizens to endure deprivation and pain. This education requires a
large measure of leisure and freedom from immediate economic needs
(4.3.12). The conditions of natural scarcity in Persia, to say nothing of
what is required to preserve the requisite austerity, make it impossible
for all, or even most, to enjoy such leisure. The majority of men cannot,
then, participate in the regime as full citizens. Thus even in the absence
of threats from abroad, the peers live under a constant necessity of
devoting themselves to the arts of war. Competition for honor proves an
effective means to attain this kind of excellence. But with competition
comes strife, and with honor some element of self-concern, not only
for the citizen's own virtue but also for its proper reward. Within the
limits set by a heartfelt patriotism, a stable if delicate balance between
the classes and among the citizens can be maintained. Because of
the nature of this balance, the republican community must remain an
essentially closed society, distrustful of change, whether technological
or political, and disdainful, even intolerant, of foreigners, with their
unfamiliar and therefore potentially corrupting ways. The example of
Cyrus, "who was said to be the greatest lover of honor and who risked
all danger for the sake of praise," will demonstrate how this love of
honor, once liberated from the narrow perspective of the republican
citizen, can undermine the very regime that fosters it (1.2.1).

Cyrus's Multicultural Education

No city, not even one located in some faraway, "barbaric place,"[53] exists
in complete isolation. Xenophon, more than any other classical thinker,

---

53. Plato *Republic* 499c–d.

is willing to explore at length the consequences of this admission.[54] The problematic relation between foreign and domestic affairs is present even in the circumstances of Cyrus's birth. The marriage between his Persian father and Median mother supports an alliance intended to preserve both peoples' security and relative independence. But not only does the strength of this alliance eventually give the Assyrians a useful justification or pretext to invade, more important, it opens the way for Cyrus to escape the full impression of the Persian laws. These laws stress the submission of the citizen to the dictates of the common good and leave little if any room for the development of natural gifts or faculties. Accordingly, the individual "Cyrus" goes unmentioned in the section of the *Cyropaedia* devoted to Persian education.

Then, at about the age of twelve, well before he has completed the necessary requirements even for the class of boys, Cyrus is summoned by his grandfather to visit him in Media. The request of an important ally and father-in-law to the king can hardly be refused. Cyrus's upbringing thus turns out to be neither wholly Persian nor wholly Median, but, like himself, a mixture or amalgam of the two. He is in many ways the product of a multicultural education some 2,500 years *avant la lettre*. Today, such an education is often advocated as a means to make us tolerant by deepening our understanding of and appreciation for the history and customs of traditions other than our own. It also holds out the promise of a better understanding of our own culture by providing different perspectives from which to examine it, perspectives that will broaden our vision and reveal as mere prejudice assumptions that had at first seemed self-evident truths. Both of these aims appear to find their full achievement in the person of Cyrus. Once freed from attachment to the fundamental assumptions of the regime into which he was born, he is entirely without national prejudice and goes on to found a multiethnic, multilingual empire (1.5 ff.; 2.2.26).

No one, however, begins life so cosmopolitan or enlightened. Part of Xenophon's purpose in describing Cyrus's life in Media is to indicate the difficulties of making such an ascent. During his early days in Media, Cyrus behaves much like any foreigner traveling away from home for the first time; he judges and weighs what he sees by the

54. Cf. the almost comic treatment of foreign relations in Plato *Republic* 450c–d, 499a–d, 540d. See also Aristotle *Politics* 1330a34–38, 1332a28–31.

standards of his native land. So long as one believes one's own way
of life to be self-sufficient and experiences it as a complete and
seamless whole, the mere existence of different ways of life does
not of itself arouse or attract interest. Consider, for example, the
Persians as described by Herodotus: they hold their own way of life
to be the best, that of their nearest neighbor second best, and so on,
ranking all foreigners in proportion to their distance from the center
of the world.[55] In Cyrus's case, his grandfather has an elaborate dinner
prepared for him so that he will not suffer so much from homesickness,
a malady, incidentally, to which he seems to be immune (1.3.4; 8.7.1).
When Astyages asks him whether the lavish dinner is better than
what they eat in Persia, Cyrus gives a surprising response: "Oh no,
Grandfather, with us the road to satiety is much more simple and
direct than with you; for among us bread and meat take us there.
Though you pursue the same goal as we, you go wandering through
many a maze, up and down, and scarcely reach the place we have long
ago arrived" (1.3.4). The Persian in Cyrus, raised on bread and cress,
assumes that one eats simply to fill the stomach. Astyages suspects, and
not without reason, that inexperience and Persian prejudice are what
keep Cyrus from appreciating how good the food really is. Xenophon
himself vouches for the superior quality of the dishes served in royal
courts and presents Cyrus as refusing the food before even tasting it
(1.3.5; 8.2.4). Some amount of experience is the necessary precondition
for making certain judgments; to reject the unfamiliar out of hand is
to constrict one's horizon unnecessarily. Cyrus's behavior smacks of
what is called today "ethnocentrism." Of course, Cyrus could have
defended his tastes on other grounds. The simplicity of the Persians'
fare, and their moderation in general, frees them from a dependence
on a vast array of cooks and bakers and the great expense of maintaining
them (8.2.6); it discourages overindulgence and preserves good health
(1.6.17); and, perhaps most important, by habituating the Persians
to short rations, it contributes to their being better soldiers, able to
withstand and triumph over the deprivations faced in war (1.2.9–11;
1.5.12).[56] Such arguments can hardly be offered by a guest, however,

55. Herodotus 1.134.
56. For the utility of ἐγκράτεια in wartime, see *Hel.* 5.3.20. Later, when the ranks
of the Persian army have been swelled with foreigners, Cyrus undertakes to duplicate

not even a favored grandchild, and especially when the host is a despot and rather fond of the pleasures of the table.[57] But over the course of the meal, Cyrus comes to understand and demonstrate yet another benefit of his self-control. After he turns down the elaborate dishes, Astyages tries to tempt him with the simpler fare of just plain meat. Cyrus accepts this food, but instead of eating it, proceeds to give it all away to those who had performed some pleasing service for him. More hungry for reputation than food, with this act of benevolence, Cyrus takes the first step toward building a loyal band of followers. Moreover, he does so in a manner that establishes an important precedent for his later career; he is most generous with what belongs to others.[58] Cyrus's behavior also demonstrates that the mere discovery that different peoples have different ways of life and value the world from different perspectives is not sufficient to call into question one's own way of life or thinking. So long as our own beliefs and practices appear entirely sound, such exposure can lead just as easily, and perhaps more surely, to condemnation and intolerance than to genuine openness and wonder. Had Cyrus returned to Persia having seen only the Medes' customs concerning food and drink, he would have gone home with some amusing stories of their peculiar ways, but otherwise little altered by his travels.

Yet Cyrus does not reject everything he sees in Media. The despot Astyages goes about according to the Median custom, wearing makeup, with colored pencil around his eyes, white lead rubbed on his face,

---

the Persian training in self-control: "In order that we not become sick from suddenly going without wine, we should do the following: Let us straight away start to drink water with our food, since by doing so we will not change very much. For whoever eats barley bread eats a cake that has already been kneaded with water, and whoever eats wheaten bread eats bread that has been mixed with water; and everything boiled has been prepared with quite a lot of water. So, if we drink wine [only] after the meal, our soul, having no less, will restore itself. But then we must also diminish our after-dinner wine until we imperceptibly become water-drinkers. For shifting little by little makes every nature bear up under changes. So the god also teaches, by leading us little by little from winter to endure the intense summer heat, and from summer's heat to the intense cold of winter. We shall [proceed] by imitating him to reach our goal by first habituating ourselves" (6.2.27; cf. *Poroi* 4.36). Cyrus's whole management of the transition from republic to empire can then be considered a self-conscious *imitatio dei*. Croesus seems to recognize it as such (7.2.9–29). See also Machiavelli's discussion of *debiti mezzi* (Machiavelli, *Discourses*, 1.41).

57. *Hiero* 1.13–15.
58. Machiavelli, *Prince*, 64.

and a wig of false hair. He also wears a purple robe and many bracelets and necklaces. When Cyrus first arrives and recognizes him as his mother's father, he immediately kisses him and declares, "Oh, Mother, how beautiful (καλός) my grandfather is." This initial admiration, an immediate attraction for something both beautiful and foreign, is what draws Cyrus most powerfully into the Median way of life. But if Mandane is pleased by the easy and natural affection between her son and his grandfather, she is no less troubled by its larger implications. Having lived in both countries, she knows that Cyrus's taste for Median sophistication in dress must eventually be accompanied by a corresponding deprecation of Persian modes. This "corruption" could prove dangerous to her son. Astyages may tolerate Cyrus's adherence to certain Persian customs at his court (1.3.14), but the Persians are unwilling and unable to accept the practice of Median ways in their country (1.5.1; 1.3.18). Mandane tries to make Cyrus see where his enthusiasm must end by asking him whom he finds more beautiful, his father or grandfather. Cyrus replies, "Of the Persians, Mother, my father is much the most beautiful (κάλλιστος); but of the Medes, as far as I have seen them in the streets or at court, my grandfather is by far the most beautiful (κάλλιστος)."[59] Cyrus's distinction between Persians and Medes and his refusal to compare them allows him to maintain that two different men are both "most beautiful." In this way he avoids making, or at least expressing, what might have been a difficult choice. He is rewarded for his cleverness with a kiss from his grandfather, a beautiful robe, bracelets, necklaces, a gold-studded bridle, and instruction in horsemanship. Cyrus is especially pleased with learning how to ride, something unknown in Persia, where the mountainous country makes it difficult to raise and maintain horses. These gifts he gladly accepts and does not give away, at least not until his return to Persia (1.4.26). Yet the tension between the two ways of life brought out by Mandane's question remains unresolved.

59. Too 1998, 289–90, claims that it is "perhaps significant" that, apart from Astyages, the only individuals described by this adjective in the *Cyropaedia* are Sacas and Panthea, "that is figures who are other than freeborn male and who are subordinate within the structure of Median tyranny." Significant or not, the adjective is here applied to Cambyses and never in the text of the *Cyropaedia* to Sacas. See 1.3.9.

When Astyages learns that Mandane is preparing to return to her husband in Persia, he asks her to leave Cyrus behind with him. Rather than oppose her father's will, she defers the decision to Cyrus. Astyages had become quite attached to the boy and tries to entice him with all kinds of extravagant promises: his bodyguard will no longer keep Cyrus from visiting when he pleases; horses and whatever else Astyages possesses will be at his disposal; he will be permitted to eat in whatever manner he wishes; the animals in the park will be his to hunt; and other children will be found as playmates. In short, Astyages concludes, "Whatever else you may desire, just ask me and you shall not fail to have it" (1.3.14). Cyrus "quickly and without hesitation" declares his wish to stay. When Mandane asks in good Persian fashion for the reasons behind his decision, his response, although qualified by Xenophon's "it is said that he said," makes no mention of his grandfather's promises. While he is the best among the children in Persia at throwing the spear and shooting the bow, he finds that here in Media he is inferior to his playmates in horsemanship. "And let me tell you, Mother, this vexes me very much." But if he stays and learns how to ride, he will still retain his excellence at the Persian exercises on foot, and will, moreover, be able to give support to his grandfather as a cavalryman if ever called upon (1.3.15). Mandane seems not to have anticipated that Cyrus would wish to stay behind, and his motives for doing so, however laudable, do nothing to quiet her worries. Her concern for her son and the future king of the Persians at last pushes her to broach a delicate subject, one particularly difficult to discuss while at her father's court. "But how, my child, will you learn justice here when your teachers are over there?" Cyrus reassures her that he already knows all about these things and recounts the lesson that taught him so thoroughly as to dispense with the need for further studies, at least under their care. In Persia,

the teacher appointed me to decide cases for the others, as being myself very exact in the knowledge of justice. Yet in one case I received a whipping for not having decided correctly. The case was this. A big boy with a small cloak put it on a small boy who had a big cloak and then took the other's for himself. When I tried the case, I thought it better that each keep the cloak that fitted him. Thereupon the teacher whipped me, saying that when I was the judge of a good fit, I should do as I had done, but when I was to judge whose cloak it was, I must examine what just possession is; whether he who took something from another by force should have it, or whether he who made or bought it should possess it. And since what is lawful is just, and force is unlawful, he commanded the judge always to render his verdict in conformity with the law. So, Mother, I understand what is just in all cases very exactly. But if I am at all deficient, my grandfather here will teach me that. (1.3.16–17)

Cyrus based his decision on a reasonable consideration of what each of the boys could best use. In this particular case, there was a common good or coincidence of interests between the two; they both benefited from the exchange. To understand the teacher's violent reaction, we must keep in mind that education in Persia is in effect restricted to the wealthy. The distinction between rich and poor constitutes a barrier to the degree to which all Persians may share in the larger common good of the political community. Of course, not every wealthy child is deserving, nor every poor child unworthy of being educated. Whatever disproportions might arise could seem to be resolved by the same method Cyrus applies to the problem of the coats: redistribution with an eye to what is fitting or most appropriate. Yet even or especially a republic like Persia, one that aims at the perfection of its citizens' virtues, must look to secure the preconditions for their cultivation and practice. Education requires a certain amount of leisure and wealth, and so the regime must ensure that at least some citizens enjoy them. But were Persia, or any other society, to recognize the legitimacy of Cyrus's decision about the coats and attempt to apply the standard of "the fitting" to the possession of all other goods, the effects would be revolutionary and disastrous. A direct appeal to what is useful or good is therefore forbidden by the laws, which unequivocally declare that just possession depends on making or buying, and that one must *always* decide according to the law. In this way, there may be particular instances of injustice that go uncorrected, but the good of the community as a whole is better preserved.[60]

Many commentators have concluded that Xenophon blithely accepts the simple equation of the just and the legal.[61] Jean Luccioni, for example, claims that "Xenophon insists on the character of absolute obligation which is attached to the principle of obedience to the laws."[62]

60. Cf. Plato *Laws* 757c–e.
61. Sinclair 1967, 90–91; Gera 1993, 74–78; Ferrari 1995, 113 n. 43.
62. Luccioni 1949, 65.

This opinion appears sound, especially since Xenophon presents his Socrates endorsing the same view on more than one occasion; and much of the defense he offers for his teacher in the *Memorabilia* rests on just this point.[63] But precisely the apologetic character of the *Memorabilia* casts doubts on its ultimate authority; the most persuasive or effective speech is by no means always the truest.[64] Here, in the less cautious *Cyropaedia*, we see that Xenophon is aware of powerful objections to such a simplistic understanding of the relation between justice and the law. And in the *Oeconomicus*, he records a conversation between Socrates and Critoboulus where they come to a conclusion quite similar to that of the young Cyrus. Utility should determine the ownership of property; a thing belongs to the one who knows how best to use it.[65] Not law or custom but knowledge turns out to determine just possession. This line of reasoning ultimately culminates in the claim that only a wise man can correctly determine who should have what in each particular case.[66] But such perfect wisdom appears to be unavailable, at least for human beings (1.6.46). Moreover, a life spent entering into others' troubles and sorting out their disputes in order to distribute everything correctly would be a life of thankless toil—that is, a most foolish life (7.5.45; 7.2.27–28; 8.2.27). For these reasons, and perhaps because the wise apparently need very little to live on,[67] it becomes tolerable to respect and even to defend the equation of the just with the legal, although in no way as an "absolute obligation."[68] But the laws, or rather those who make and enforce them, cannot afford to make these, or any other, roundabout arguments in their defense, since their respectability and power depend in large measure on a

63. E.g., *Mem.* 4.4.1, 1.1.17.
64. *Cyro.* 1.6.10; *Mem.* 4.6.15.
65. *Oec.* 1.5ff., 6.4.
66. These are essentially the same arguments about property that lie behind Socrates' conversations with Cephalus and Polemarchus in the *Republic*. There Socrates pushes them to their extremes and institutes absolute communism under the rule of philosopher kings, a result not without its comic implications (cf. Aristophanes' *Assembly of Women*). Yet this regime is ambiguously good, especially for the wise, and they must be "compelled" to rule. It seems that even the best men "prefer to be benefited rather than take the trouble to benefit others" (Plato *Republic* 347d, 519d). Cf. *Cyro.* 7.2.27–28.
67. Cf. 1.3.17 with ἀχίτων at *Mem.* 1.6.3.
68. *Oec.* 2.8; *Apol.* 28. Aristotle *Politics* 1269a8–12; 1286a9–16. Strauss 1970, 95–97.

belief among the citizens in the validity of an absolute obligation. The
"teachers" therefore make no arguments whatsoever and enforce such
a general belief with beatings and threats of other punishment (cf.
2.2.14). That the distinction between lawful possession and force is
itself maintained at bottom by force is a lesson not likely to have been
missed by Cyrus, when he was beaten for having undertaken to benefit
his fellows.[69]

Whatever else one might say about the reactions of Xenophon's
commentators, Cyrus's mother is troubled by his simple equation of
the just and the legal. The formulation does nothing to address the
difficulty that so worries her—namely, that the same things are not
everywhere considered lawful. In Media, Astyages has made himself
despot over all; in Persia, equality is established to be just. Cambyses
may be king of the Persians, but he is the first to accept and do
whatever the city commands. Not his soul or will (ψυχή), but the law is
the standard of justice there.[70] These different views are ultimately
bound to come into conflict, as they do now: should Cyrus return to
complete his education in accordance with the Persian laws, or stay in
Media as Astyages wishes? Cyrus's assurance that he already possesses
a thorough understanding of justice, combined with his expressed
willingness to learn whatever little remains from his grandfather, only
heighten Mandane's concerns. "How will you not be beaten to death
when you come home if you arrive having learned not kingship but
tyranny, according to which it is thought that one ought to have more
than all others" (τὸ πλεῖον οἴεσθαι χρῆναι πάντων ἔχειν)? Cyrus is
ready with a response. He claims that Astyages is in fact much better at
teaching others to have less than to have more (πλεῖον ἔχειν), because
he has taught all the Medes to have less. "So take heart, your father will
not send me or anyone else away who will have learned to take unfair
advantage" (πλεονεκτεῖν, 1.3.18). Cyrus's argument assumes that he
is as unlikely to learn tyranny from a tyrant as moderation from the
example of the Persian elders. Yet much of the education he has already
been given presupposes and encourages the belief that virtue can be
taught by imitation. And Cyrus has already shown himself eager to
follow his grandfather in matters of dress and adornment (1.2.8; 1.3.3,

69. Gera 1993, 74, notes an echo of Herodotus 1.114–15 in this story.
70. Cf. *CL* 15.7.

10). Mandane remains troubled, and further discussion apparently ensues. "But, at last, his mother went away, and Cyrus stayed and was brought up there"(1.4.1). What remains unclear is whether Mandane allowed him to stay because her fears were allayed or increased by their conversation. For his part, Cyrus soon excels his Median playmates in horsemanship, but does not, for that reason, then think to return home (1.4.5 with 1.3.15).

If Cyrus's stay in Media causes him to miss a good part of the Persian education, his time at Astyages' court does permit a fuller development of his natural faculties than would have been possible under the strict supervision of the Persian laws. We noted earlier that among the barbarians, Cyrus is said to be the most beautiful, the most benevolent, the greatest lover of learning, and the most ambitious. Xenophon now amends that account by removing the superlatives when speaking in his own name: that is, Cyrus is a lover of honor, a lover of learning, and benevolent. As for being the most beautiful, Xenophon says instead that he is "a lover of beauty," a change that might well explain Cyrus's interest in cosmetics and other adornment (1.3.3; 1.4.3; cf. 1.2.1).[71] But, whatever their extent, the greater freedom from conventional restraints in Media allows him to exercise his benevolence and ambition without the same risk of being beaten for his efforts.

Cyrus's benevolence first shows itself within the sphere of his immediate family. When Astyages falls ill, Cyrus waits day and night upon his every need and pleasure. "He never left his side nor ceased to weep, but clearly showed to all that he greatly feared lest his grandfather die." When he recovers, there is then no favor Astyages can refuse Cyrus if he should ask it of him (1.4.2).[72] Among his companions, Cyrus's benevolence takes the form of visiting their fathers and showing such kindnesses as he can; if any of them have need of something from the king, he makes every effort to secure it. Yet, on at least one occasion, Cyrus's care for his companions goes well beyond tending to their present needs to inspiring them with new hopes and desires. He so loves to hunt that he quickly kills all the animals in his grandfather's park. Astyages learns of this and allows Cyrus to go with his uncle to hunt in the wild. When they first hap-

---

71. Cf. 8.3.14; *Oec.* 10.2–9.
72. Cf. 1.3.14. Astyages is apparently as little bound by his word as by the law.

pen upon some game, Cyrus is so overcome with enthusiasm that he charges the most dangerous animals against the explicit instructions of his uncle. Upon Cyrus's return, Astyages rebukes him for needlessly risking his life. Cyrus, unchastened, distributes the game to his companions, describing in poetic language the excitement of the hunt: "The deer leaped skyward as if on wings, and the boars came charging as they say brave men do in battle." He concludes by asking whether their fathers might permit them to go on a hunt too. "Easily," they reply, "if Astyages should order it." Here lies Cyrus's problem. His grandfather has just rebuked him, and he now claims he can no longer chatter and coax for things as before. Xenophon confirms this, reporting that Cyrus was at that age when he was bashful and blushed whenever in the presence of his elders (1.4.4). The boys are naturally disappointed. "What you're telling us is bad. But if you're not able to act for us when needed, we shall just have to ask someone else." Cyrus is stung by their ingratitude and storms off in silence to plan his next move. Finally, he summons up his daring and confronts Astyages with his wish. As expected, Astyages refuses. Only after Cyrus sulks about for some time, silent and sullen-faced, does he relent and himself take his grandson out to hunt with his companions. The expedition is such a success that he resolves to take Cyrus out whenever possible, and, "for the sake of Cyrus," to bring the other boys as well (1.4.5–15).

In ways such as this, Cyrus demonstrates his care for others. But as Astyages perceives and Cyrus's anger at his playmates' ingratitude confirms, his benevolence is far from self-forgetting. His deeds are all calculated to increase his honor or influence.[73] Even in the care that Cyrus takes of the sick Astyages, Xenophon stresses the public character of his attentions, of the tears he makes clear to all and from which he receives no little profit. But if Xenophon makes manifest the connection between Cyrus's benevolence and his love of honor in a way that makes them virtually indistinguishable, this element of self-interest, however large, does not meet with any explicit disapproval. He closes his account of this part of Cyrus's life with the following

---

73. For an unusually explicit statement of the true character of Cyrus's benevolence, see 8.2.1.

tribute: "In this way Cyrus passed most of his time, being the cause of pleasure and some good to all, and of bad to no one"(1.4.15).[74]

Cyrus's situation in Media changes dramatically when he is fifteen or sixteen. At this time, the son of the neighboring Assyrian king makes a surprise raid on the Medes. Astyages rushes to the frontier with his forces; Cyrus, on his own initiative, puts on armor for the first time and joins the soldiers. Astyages is surprised to see him in the field but allows him to stay by his side. The Medes find themselves unable to counterattack the raiding parties because of the Assyrians' superior tactical position. Cyrus, however, immediately sees a way to outmaneuver them. Amazed at his watchfulness and prudence, Astyages takes his advice and orders his son, Cyaxares, to charge. Cyrus, again on his own initiative, quickly puts himself at the head of this force and leads it to rout an enemy very much surprised to find that the Medes no longer fight according to their "habitual fashion" (1.4.16–23).

Cyrus's actions in battle, unlike his earlier works of benevolence, cannot simply be reduced to a calculation of how best to win honor. However "prudent and wide awake" he is before the engagement, once the fighting begins, he is "like a well-bred but inexperienced hound, rushing in without foresight against a boar," unable to contain his cries of joy and mad with daring (μαινόμενον τῇ τόλμῃ). Even in the aftermath, "as the others were going home, he alone did nothing but ride around and gaze [ἐθεᾶτο] at the fallen. Only with difficulty did those assigned to do so manage to drag him away and lead him to Astyages. And as he came, he sent his escort well before him, because he saw that his grandfather's face was angry on account of his [Cyrus's] gazing [at the corpses] [τῇ θέα τῇ αὐτοῦ]"(1.4.24). Cyrus clearly enjoys the fight itself and especially looking at the fallen. His "theoretical" tastes and ambitions appear to be in perfect harmony with the requirements of service to a particular political community.[75] After the battle, he is celebrated "in story and in song" as the cause of the Medes' victory. Yet no more can Xenophon say of Cyrus that he was a cause of good to all and harm to none. His service to the Medes puts him at odds not only with the Assyrians but with the Persians to a certain

74. Cf. Plato *Republic* 335c–e.
75. Plato *Republic* 439e–440a; cf. 375c.

extent as well. Persian law unequivocally states that a citizen must not
go to war until the age of twenty-five (1.2.13; cf. 1.6.33–34). Indeed,
Cyrus's reward, his increasing fame, is what alerts his father to this
violation and prompts him to send orders for his son to return and
complete his formal education. Xenophon reports that "it is said that
Cyrus said" he wished to go home so that his father would not be
annoyed or the city blame him. "Astyages, too, thought it necessary
to send him away," Xenophon reports somewhat more reliably. If he
admired Cyrus before, "he was now completely astonished by him"
(τότε ὑπερεξεπέπληκτο ἐπ᾽ αὐτῷ). For good or ill, Cyrus's growing
stature threatens to eclipse that of his uncle, Cyaxares, Astyages' legitimate heir, and might well present a challenge to an orderly succession.
Cyrus does, however, seem well on his way to fulfilling Astyages' hope
that he will prove to be "a man able both to benefit his friends and
harm his enemies," although his status as a member of two different communities makes it more difficult than usual to delineate the
boundaries of these categories (1.4.25).

Opportunity

After returning to Persia, Cyrus spends one more year in the class of
boys before passing into that of the youths. At first his classmates tease
him, thinking he must have learned to live a life of soft pleasures among
the Medes. But when they see that he eats and drinks Persian fare with
as much relish as themselves, and sometimes even gives part of his own
share away,[76] they once again assent to his superiority. So little does
his time in Media appear to have changed him that he soon gains
a reputation for preeminence in attention to his duties, endurance,
respect for his elders, and obedience to the magistrates. Cyrus told
one of his admirers in Media that he would soon return there (1.4.28).
Yet over ten years go by before he can fulfill this promise. Once back in
Persia, the individual Cyrus again disappears, and the remainder of his
interrupted education is related by Xenophon in one brief sentence.
He might well have spent his entire life in similar obscurity had not
events outside of Persia conspired to threaten the republic's existence.

76. Cf. *CL* 15.4.

About the time Cyrus finishes his formal education and passes into the class of peers, Astyages dies and Cyaxares succeeds to the Median throne. The Assyrian king, having just subdued several peoples, and perhaps emboldened by Astyages' demise, turns his thoughts to further expansion, calculating that if he can conquer the Medes, he will easily rule all the rest. Some of the Assyrian's allies join him on account of the gifts and money he provides; others seem to be persuaded by his argument that the united power of the Medes and Persians must be opposed before they start to subjugate their neighbors one by one (1.5.3). The alliance intended to secure the mutual safety and independence of Persia and Media thus also serves to facilitate the Assyrian king's imperial ambitions. Nor can we dismiss his argument as mere pretext or subterfuge and his allies' compliance as gullibility. Events prove such fears to be altogether justified.[77]

As soon as Cyaxares learns of the Assyrian's intentions, he sends to Persia for troops and requests that his nephew be sent at their head. The Persian elders elect Cyrus general of the army and order him to choose 200 peers, who are each to select four more. To these 1,000 peers, 30,000 commoners are added to serve as targeteers, slingers, and bowmen. After the peers have all been chosen, Cyrus calls them together and delivers the first public speech of his career. He begins by explaining to the peers why he has chosen them. "I have seen that from boyhood on you have enthusiastically done what the city believes to be noble and held back from what it considers base" (1.5.7). In other words, they have fulfilled the requirements of Persian education. Cyrus seems, then, to be guided by this traditional judgment of a man's worth. Yet when it comes to explaining his own willingness to accept his post, his motives turn out to be anything but conventional. We might expect the man reputed to surpass his contemporaries in obedience to rulers and respect for his elders to make some mention of his hereditary duties or special election by the Council. Instead, he makes a most extraordinary statement, one whose subversive and revolutionary character can be fully grasped only when understood in the context of the great political power and prestige afforded in Persia to tradition and hence the elders: "I have come to understand that our ancestors were no worse than

77. Cf. *Hel.* 5.2.38–39; Thucydides 1.2.5–6.

we are." That is, they were also not necessarily better. Cyrus does
not begin from the generally accepted assumption of their superiority.
Following this rather surprising assertion of the likely equality between
their forefathers and themselves, and thus between the young and
the old, Cyrus goes on to claim that the ancestral ways are in fact
somewhat foolish and should therefore be abandoned, or, at the very
least, substantially modified. "They too spent their time practicing
(ἀσκοῦντες) the very deeds that are held to be virtue. But what good
thing they acquired by being such [men], either for the community
of Persians or themselves, I am no longer able to see." Whereas the
Persians have held that virtue is to be practiced for its own sake, Cyrus
now declares that "no virtue is practiced by human beings so that those
who become upright (ἐσθλοί) should not get more than the wicked"
(1.5.7–9). Likewise breaking with the traditional Persian methods of
instruction, he supports his position with arguments and illustrations.

Cyrus begins his demonstration with an attack on the traditional
understanding and practice of continence (ἐγκράτεια), the foundation
of the other virtues, or, in the spirit of his account, what might be
better characterized as the basement.[78] No one in his right mind, he
argues, abstains from enjoyment simply for the sake of abstaining, but
rather does so for the sake of some greater enjoyment in the future.
When practiced for its own sake, continence is indistinguishable from
senseless repression; alone it serves no end.[79] Cyrus supports this
argument with four examples. Those who desire to be clever speakers
do so not in order never to cease speaking well but to accomplish many
and great deeds through persuasion.[80] Similarly, those who practice the
military arts toil at them not in order never to cease fighting but to
attain great wealth, happiness, and honor both for themselves and
the city. A man who acts otherwise resembles someone who, trying
to be a good farmer, sows and cultivates a field, but then leaves the
crops unharvested, or an athlete who trains for victory only to refuse to
compete (1.5.9–11). Cyrus's first example, "clever speakers" (οἵ δεινοὶ

---

78. *Mem.* 1.5.4.

79. This view of continence was already at work in Cyrus's selection of his men.
He chose those who "enthusiastically did what the city held to be noble and held
back from what it considered base." Enthusiasm for restraint was not a criterion (cf.
2.2.13–16).

80. Cf. 5.5.46 for a later shift in Cyrus's standard for evaluating speakers.

λέγειν), might seem somewhat out of place inasmuch as rhetoric, the art of persuasive speech, forms no part of the Persian education.[81] Yet, precisely because Cyrus is himself attempting to persuade the peers by means of this unfamiliar art, he begins by reassuring them that it aims at something honorable, "the achievement of many and great goods."[82] Military exercises and athletics are of course well known to the peers, although here too Cyrus's characterization is somewhat exaggerated and misleading. This distortion becomes apparent by reflecting on his choice of what seems to be another inappropriate metaphor, his comparison of the peers to farmers.[83] Farming forms even less a part of the peers' education than does clever speaking, although their superiority in military matters allows them to force the commoners to do this work for them. But this means, contrary to Cyrus's earlier assertion, that the peers have profited, and do still profit, in some way from their practice of virtue.[84] He can pass over this advantage in silence for two reasons. First, since it rests chiefly on the peers' superiority in force, it is at odds with their declared principles of equality, merit, and the rule of law. A more or less open admission of the true basis of their rule would, of course, instruct the commoners in the necessary means to overthrow it. More important, such an avowal would also deprive the peers of their belief in the justice, and hence the legitimacy, of their rule. Second, the advantage that they do enjoy falls well short of giving them the "great wealth, happiness, and honor" that Cyrus thinks their military strength could enable them to acquire. Insofar as the necessity of keeping the commoners in check compels them to remain at home and hence moderates the scope and profitability of their talents, there is something to this insight.[85] At

81. Cf. *Mem.* 1.2.46.

82. The first half of Cyrus's speech in fact follows a procedure similar to that of the Unjust Speech in Aristophanes' *Clouds* (see esp. 1060–62).

83. Cyrus speaks of those who actually engage in military exercises and athletics, but refers more abstractly to those "desiring" to be good speakers and farmers, because these skills form no part of the peers' education.

84. Cf. 2.1.3, 7.5.79. The Spartan boast "It is not by caring for the fields but by caring for ourselves that we come to possess the fields" (Plutarch *Moralia* 217a) could just as well have been made by a Persian peer.

85. Thucydides (8.24, 8.40) suggests a similar explanation of the remarkable moderation practiced by the Spartans and Chians even in times of "peace." See Rahe 1994, 126 n. 45; Orwin 1994, 83–85, 200.

the moment, the Persians are certainly poorer, less feared, and less admired by the world than their allies, the Medes (1.5.2).

If Cyrus openly attacks the understanding of continence as something to be practiced for its own sake, he does not dismiss or abandon the virtue altogether. He himself moderately holds back from applying his analysis of continence to the other Persian virtues, and does so with a clear end in sight. The events that place Cyrus at the head of the Persian army, that put him in a position to criticize the ancestral ways and even undermine the whole spirit of the traditional Persian education, also compel him to mitigate or soften the full force of his polemical critique. Persia is, after all, threatened by attack from without; and an army completely demoralized by the inadequacy of its previous training would be of little use. He turns, then, in the remainder of his speech to praise those parts of the peers' education that he still considers reliable or sound. Speaking on the authority of his experience abroad, Cyrus assures the peers that their task will not be difficult: they are like professional soldiers marching against rank amateurs. If the enemy are admittedly strong in managing their bows and spears and horses, they nonetheless lack the Persians' capacity to endure toil, sleeplessness, hunger, and thirst. Moreover, the peers carry in their souls "that most noble and warlike possession.... You rejoice in being praised more than in anything else, and lovers of praise must of necessity submit to every labor and risk every danger with pleasure" (1.5.12).

Whatever the shortcomings of their enemies and the merits of physical endurance and the love of praise, to see that Cyrus overstates their importance, we need only consider his offhand treatment of the enemy's superiority in cavalry, the most glaring defect in the present Persian army (1.4.4; 1.3.15; 1.6.10; 4.3ff.), and compare it with the decisive role the Persian cavalry will eventually play in their ultimate success (e.g., 7.1.19). Cyrus, too, anticipates that some of his men may doubt the veracity of his account and accordingly offers proof of his good faith: "If I say anything while knowing the contrary to be the case, I deceive myself. For if you fail to be such as I say, your shortcomings will fall on me" (1.5.13). As general, his interests and the army's are one. For this reason, they can trust him wholeheartedly.[86]

86. Consider, however, the fate of the Lydian general, Croesus, at 7.2 ff., as well as Cyrus's remarks at 5.2.23.

In their ignorance of the outside world, the peers may accept Cyrus's assessment of their relative worth. But the true foundation of his own confidence must lie elsewhere, perhaps in a just estimate of his own considerable talents. After all, as a mere boy of sixteen, without military experience or rank, he was the cause of a Median victory over these same Assyrians. But, independent of purely military considerations, Cyrus might also consider this moment worth the greatest of risks because it affords the rare opportunity to "corrupt" or transform the peers' traditional understanding of virtue with little danger of their immediately questioning in turn their own justice and nobility. Cyrus exploits the situation by appealing to what are admittedly contingent standards, but ones that exercise great power over the law-bred and communal spirits of the peers. "Let us set out with confidence since the appearance of wanting [to take] the possessions of others unjustly is far from us. For now our enemies are coming as unjust aggressors, and our friends call us to help. And what is more just than defending ourselves, or more noble than aiding our friends?"

James Tatum, a commentator otherwise sensitive to the practical necessities governing Cyrus's imperial ambitions, judges this first public speech a failure on two separate grounds. First, inasmuch as he considers the speech a "straightforward" praise of Persian education, he thinks it encourages a dangerous complacency in the face of a formidable enemy.[87] Second, and more accurately, he maintains that the speech "is idealistic and quite uncontaminated by practical observation or preparation for actual battle."[88] Yet Tatum overlooks those aspects of the speech strongly critical of the Persian education, and ignores the fact that military necessities are not always the first or highest necessities, especially for a general who has in mind something more than the usual kind of war. The speech in fact provides the strongest possible evidence in support of Machiavelli's judgment that Cyrus ranks among the great founder-prophets who establish not only new states but new moral orders and ways of life.[89] Toward the end of the *Eudemian Ethics*, Aristotle distinguishes between virtue practiced

---

87. The French commentator Marcel Bizos (1971, 35 n. 2) finds to the contrary that "une telle assurance avant le combat est de bonne tactique psychologique."
88. Tatum 1989, 83–84.
89. Machiavelli *Prince*, 24.

for its own sake and virtue practiced for the sake of external goods. The
latter, political in character, is the virtue "possessed by the Spartans and
others like them."[90] Certainly, the ease with which Cyrus introduces
this new understanding and the rapidity of its acceptance by the peers,
provide some grounds for wondering whether their original conception and practice of virtue ever possessed a solid foundation.[91] Were
it not for the astonishing universalism implicit in Cyrus's approach to
politics (2.2.26), a universalism famously lacking in Sparta's policies,[92]
this lowering of the aim of political life in Persia would appear to
represent the simple corruption or descent of Xenophon's republican
ideal back into the practices of that city. What remains to be seen
is whether Cyrus's understanding of virtue pursued for the sake of
wealth, happiness, and honor on a global scale can provide a superior
or sustainable alternative to the traditional morality he supplants.

90. Aristotle *Eudemian Ethics* 1248b38–49a17.
91. Bruell 1987, 97, 99.
92. Machiavelli, *Discourses*, 1.6.3.

Chapter Two

Transformation

Infantry

The transformation of the Persian army from a relatively small defensive force into a larger, more acquisitive power, a change implied if not explicitly stated in Cyrus's new understanding of virtue, is facilitated if not made altogether necessary by the Assyrian's aggression. Cyrus arrives in Media alone and well ahead of the army in order to consult with his uncle on the precise character of the military situation. He tells Cyaxares that he is bringing 20,000 of the commoners and an unspecified number of peers (2.1.2). Modern editors of the Greek text universally emend this to 30,000 in order to make the figure agree with the number of commoners actually sent (1.5.6). However, the figure 20,000 is found in all the manuscripts and is also the number Cyrus uses in a later passage when calculating with Cyaxares the size of their combined forces (2.1.6). The usual emendation neither corrects a lapse on the part of Xenophon nor removes a corruption in the original text. Rather, it creates an additional impediment to a genuine appreciation of the character of Xenophon's writing. Not only does Cyrus decline to give his ally and commander an accurate count of the number of peers (either those in the army or left behind at home),[1] he intentionally underestimates the number of commoners, and this even before learning the true extent of the enemy forces. His own long-term, if unstated, plan requires that the commoners be armed; and Cyaxares is the only one who can be made to bear the necessary

---

1. Cyrus's guarded response as to the actual number of peers recalls the similar care the Spartans took to keep the number of their citizens secret (Thucydides 5.68).

expense. The more desperate Cyrus can make their situation appear, the easier his task of persuasion will be. Thus the very first word out of his mouth when he arrives in Media is but the first of many deceptions he will practice on his uncle.[2] In Cyrus's hands, his father's counsel to be on guard against Cyaxares' lies turns out to have another and more offensive application (1.6.9; cf. 1.6.38).

When Cyrus and Cyaxares do add up the expected number of men on each side, they find that the Persians and Medes face what appears to be an impossible situation. Cyrus may boast of the abilities of the peers—"even though they are few, these so-called peers easily rule over the very numerous Persians" (2.1.3; cf. 8.1.4)—but this superiority is not enough to overcome the overwhelming material advantages of the Assyrian forces. They estimate the strength of the Assyrians and their allies at 60,000 horse, 200,000 foot soldiers, and 100 chariots. The Medes and Persians, if joined by the Armenians, will have 14,000 horse and 100,000 foot soldiers. So long as both sides fight in their customary manner, victory will go to the one with greater numbers (2.1.5–8).[3] The only response Cyaxares can imagine is to send to Persia for a larger force. Cyrus assures him that even if all the Persians were to come, the allies would still be outnumbered by the enemy.[4] Instead, he proposes a change in tactics. If Cyaxares provides the commoners with the kind of weapons the peers have for fighting at close quarters, the Persians will be able to face those among the enemy who stand their ground and leave the Medes' cavalry to pursue those who flee. This strategy so appeals to Cyaxares that he no longer even thinks about sending for more Persian troops and sets about preparing the new arms. Cyrus, for his part, is left to figure out how to persuade the peers to approve the decision to arm 30,000 commoners, one he makes without consulting either them or the authorities back in Persia. No doubt the desperate military situation goes a long way toward justifying this measure. But this necessity alone does not explain why

2. See Machiavelli, *Discourses*, 2.13.1.
3. Cf. *Poroi* 4.42.
4. As there are 89,000 Persians left at home, what Cyrus says is technically true. One should note, however, that his refusal to send for more troops at the moment when their fortunes are lowest does not stop Cyrus from sending for another army from home at a time when the Assyrian threat is greatly diminished (4.5.16, 31; cf. 3.2.29).

Cyrus proposes to arm only the Persian commoners, since it would be equally, if not more, expedient to arm at least some of the more numerous Medes as well.[5]

The new weapons are ready by the time the Persian army arrives, and Cyrus calls the peers together in order to explain his plan to them. He makes no mention of the serious danger posed to Media and Persia by the overwhelming numbers of the enemy but begins with an even more direct appeal, expressing the apprehension he felt for the peers' own safety while they were making the journey to Media. Cyrus exaggerates the immediate threat and claims he feared the army might have encountered a large number of the enemy (2.1.10 with 2.1.30). Had this happened, the commoners, armed only for fighting at a distance, would have been unable to help them. To remedy this danger, their fellow countrymen, who lack nothing in bodily strength, are now to be given arms like those of the peers. The only difficulty, Cyrus claims, is that the souls of the commoners will need to be whetted for war. This will be the task of the peers: "For it belongs to an officer not only to prove himself good, but he must also take care that those under his rule will be the best possible" (2.1.11; cf. 1.6.7). What the peers believe the Persian regime does for them (1.2.15), Cyrus will now have them do for the commoners, although without the benefit of the traditional laws.[6] The peers are pleased with the proposal, believing it to mean that they will now go into battle with more support. And as Cyrus has stressed the apparent defects in the commoners' souls, they quite likely remain confident that they will continue without much difficulty to rule these lesser men. So eager are they to enlist the commoners' help, and perhaps no less conscious of the suspicions they will have to overcome in their new comrades, the peers agree to the suggestion of an anonymous speaker who proposes that the commoners receive this offer from Cyrus himself.[7] Coming from him, the most powerful and esteemed among them, it will be all the more pleasing; and as the son of

---

5. This will in fact become Cyrus's policy, but only after all of the commoners with him are armed (2.2.26).

6. Cf. τῷ αἰτίῳ at 5.4.14 for the further progression away from the Persian regime. See n. 56 to chapter 1.

7. See 8.4.11 for the probable identification of this peer as Chrysantas.

their king, his promise will be better trusted.[8] Cyrus willingly agrees
(2.1.11–12).

Before extending the invitation to the commoners, Cyrus has the
weapons brought in and set before them. To persuade the peers, Cyrus
first spoke of the danger of an enemy attack. With the commoners,
he takes a different approach; after all, they might not regard such
an attack as altogether unwelcome. He begins by implicitly depre-
cating the peers' education. He argues that the commoners' bodies
can be no worse than those of the peers, they having been born in
the same country. As for their souls, whose shortcomings he stressed
when addressing the peers, Cyrus now simply states that "it is not
fitting" (οὐδὲν προσήκει) for them to be any worse than those of the
peers (2.1.15, 11). It would of course be imprudent to remind the
commoners of their defects when soliciting their aid.[9] But this gloss
creates its own problems. If the members of the two classes are essentially equal, why is it that they live such different lives? Cyrus's
explanation runs as follows: "Even though you are as I say, you did
not share equally in the fatherland, not because you were excluded
by us, but because necessity (ἀνάγκη) compelled you to provide the
provisions." If this rather frank admission of the commoners' hard
lot falls short as an explanation of just how or why the peers avoided
sharing in their fate, Cyrus's argument does have the virtue of denying, or at least mitigating, the peers' responsibility for that situation,
and, more important, in doing so, it points toward the grounds for a
possible reconciliation between the two classes. First, necessity, being
blameless, excuses. The peers, after all, did not create the natural
scarcity that reigns in Persia. And, second, such a formulation allows for a quick and effective solution. Cyrus is now in a position,
with the help of the gods (2.1.14)—to say nothing of Cyaxares' treasury (2.1.10, 2.4.9)—to abate or even remove this "necessity." Once
eliminated, it will no longer be the cause of unjust inequality among
equals. Cyrus concludes by telling the commoners that they are to
receive the same arms, run the same risks in battle, and, something

---

8. For reasons why the commoners might have legitimate concerns on this score,
consider Thucydides 4.80. For the Spartan use of Helots in time of war, see Willetts
1954, 27–32; Cartledge 1987, 40; Hunt 1998, 13–25, 115–20.

9. Moreover, it is much easier to deceive human beings about the true character
of their souls than of their bodies (*Mem.* 2.6.12, 32).

he somehow failed to mention in his speech to the peers, "be considered worthy of similar rewards" (2.1.15). By a certain blurring of the facts on both sides (i.e., the shortcomings of the commoners' souls and the extent of the peers' culpability for those shortcomings), Cyrus begins to effect a reconciliation between the two classes, although admittedly only under pressure of a foreign threat and with Cyaxares' money.

To think that the commoners will fight as well as those who have been training all their lives is, of course, absurd (cf. 3.3.51–59; 7.1.33–34). Even Cyrus admits as much were the battle to be fought with spears and bows. The commoners are little practiced with these weapons and therefore much less adept. But the new weapons for fighting at close quarters require far less skill to master, or so Cyrus claims. He points out that the commoners are already accustomed to carrying a shield on the left arm; and when striking with a short sword in one's right hand, the target is so large and close that it is impossible to miss. Cyrus does grant that there might remain some difference between the two classes with regard to boldness or daring (τολμή, 2.1.17; cf. 7.5.76). But he denies that this constitutes a real difficulty and once again asserts that "it is not fitting" for the commoners to be any less eager than the peers; and eagerness is somewhat akin to daring. "Victory," Cyrus explains, "gives and preserves all good and noble things."[10] As the commoners hardly need to be reminded, among the good and noble things given are the possessions of the weaker (3.3.45). And if, at the moment, they have few things to preserve, this only makes them all the more eager for gain.[11] No commoner is compelled to change his place, yet all accept the offer willingly. Indeed, they believe that anyone who passes up this opportunity deserves to live in want for all

---

10. When addressing the whole of his troops, the Assyrian king takes up the same kind of arguments that Cyrus makes to the commoners. "It would be foolish for those who wish to conquer to flee and turn their blind, unarmed and handless [backs] to the enemy. And it would be foolish if one who wished to live should try to flee, knowing that the victors save themselves, while those who flee are more often killed than those who stand fast. And if anyone is eager for wealth, he too is foolish to submit to defeat. For who does not know that the victors both preserve what is their own and take in addition what belongs to the defeaated, while the defeated throw away both themselves and all that they have?" (3.3.45).

11. *Hipparchicus* 9.4: "Need brings forth great eagerness."

time to come, an implicit judgment on what they take to be the justice of their previous condition (2.1.19).[12]

Cyrus uses "the time that the enemy was said to be approaching but had not yet arrived" to develop the commoners' strength and endurance, to instruct them in the basics of military tactics, and to whet their souls for victory. To encourage obedience, willingness to toil and face danger, good discipline, and love of honor, he institutes contests among the various divisions, much as was done in the education of the youths and boys back in Persia (1.2.12, 6.2.4). There, the strife such rivalry can spawn was kept in check among the peers in part by the unspoken fear of the commoners, and in part by the instruction in continence, moderation, and justice, which was in turn supported by love of fatherland and a sure conviction of the superiority of their way of life. For the army as a whole, fear of the Assyrians now plays the role that the peers' fear of the commoners previously played in the Persian regime. But the other qualities that held the regime together are more difficult to replace or reproduce. For instance, the peers' long instruction in justice cannot be administered in the field, nor is it even possible in the Persians' view to give this training to men of the commoners' age (1.6.33–34). In its place, Cyrus has the two classes mixed together and billeted in large tents of 100 men each. This allows the men to become familiar with one another and encourages the development in them of a useful sense of shame. As for mutual devotion, having observed that animals that feed together long for one another if separated, Cyrus institutes large common meals,[13] an arrangement that has the added benefit of allowing the commoners to see for themselves that the provisions are shared out equally, regardless of class (2.1.20–31).

To announce the rule of equality in speech, even to remove the legal and economic barriers to the advancement of merit, cannot be confused with actually establishing it in practice. Cyrus may depre-

---

12. Hunt 1998, 147–53, maintains on the basis of *Cyro.* 7.5.78–79 that Cyrus opposes arming slaves for military service, a policy that Xenophon reconsiders in the *Poroi.* But Hunt neglects the similarity of the Persian commoners to Sparta's Helots, as well as the difference between Cyrus's policy before and after the establishment of his empire.

13. Cf. Xenophon's judgment of Lycurgus's famous legislation concerning these matters in the light cast by this passage. Cf. 7.1.30, *CL* 5.2–6.

cate the peers' education when speaking before the commoners, but
its advantages are all too apparent in the army's training exercises.
The peers cannot help but laugh at their new comrades' overly literal
and sheeplike obedience to orders or their rather graceless and self-
defeating insistence on strict equality with regard to the portions of
meat they now receive (2.2.1–10). Yet the discrepancy between the
official proclamation of equality and the actual situation in the field,
while providing these and other comic scenes, creates a serious, because potentially divisive, problem for the army. The peers, by reason
of their training, really are better soldiers; in the first engagement with
the enemy it is their skills that win the victory.[14] But if the soldiers
are all to share equally in everything, including the spoils of war, it is
precisely the peers who will lose an important incentive to fight their
best, and even the most capable of the commoners will have less cause
to push themselves to the extreme of excellence. So long as the Persians understood virtue to be practiced for its own sake, this difficulty
could perhaps be more easily ignored or overlooked. But now that
they consider virtue primarily as a means to honor, wealth, and other
goods, the proper distribution of these rewards becomes much more
important. Should some soldiers still fight their best and show outstanding bravery, be it from habit, duty, or some chance necessity, an
equal distribution of rewards could not help but give rise to dangerous
resentments and discontent. This is precisely the sentiment behind
the objection Chrysantas raises in a discussion with his fellow peers:
"Cyrus and all [you] present here, I have in mind that while some
of those with us are better, others merit less. Yet if something good
comes to us they [the commoners] will all consider themselves worthy
of an equal share. But I believe there is nothing more unequal among
human beings than for the good and bad to be rewarded [with] equal

14. On the eve of the new soldiers' first deployment, Cyrus reminds a soldier who
claims to be the least able of the peers: "Do not do as you sometimes do on account of
your love of hunting, Chrysantas, for you often go the whole night without sleep.
But you now must allow the men to rest a moderate amount so they might be able
to fight off sleep. Nor, because you are used to wander up and down the mountains
without human guides, and to run after the game wherever it leads you, do not now go
along paths that are hard to walk, but order your guides to lead along the easiest road,
unless it is much longer. And do not, because you are used to it, lead at a run. Go with
middling speed, in a way that the army will be capable of following you" (2.4.26–28;
cf. 5.4.17).

shares"(2.2.18).[15] Chrysantas does not push this claim to its extreme or logical conclusion; even he makes no objection to the equal sharing of provisions by all alike, a tacit admission that strict equality among unequals does have its place as a means of fostering a sense of common cause or community.[16] As Plato's Athenian Stranger observes, "There is truth in the old saying 'equality produces friendship.'"[17] But when it comes to the distribution of honors and spoils, which are, after all, what most of the soldiers are now fighting for, equality falls too far short of justice not to arouse great indignation. This practice therefore serves to undermine the spirit and efficacy of the army's best men. On the other hand, to give rewards commensurate with merit would, with rare exceptions, only serve to perpetuate the previous and now admittedly defective order. It is precisely for the latter reason that Chrysantas believes the commoners will never willingly accept such a policy. He appeals to Cyrus to establish this rule by fiat, much as he did when laying down rules for the various contests he instituted.

Cyrus supports Chrysantas's proposal but declines to establish it himself. He points out that while the men do not yet dispute the justice of what he does by his authority as general and with the funds he has brought from home, this will not be the case with any spoils that they acquire by fighting. These things will be considered as common property. Moreover, neither he nor the peers are in a position to dictate terms to the newly armed commoners. Their consent has become essential. Cyrus therefore proposes that they call a council to deliberate on the matter in public, assuring the peers that even the commoners will think it shameful for those who serve the community best not to receive the highest rewards. His confidence turns out to be well founded. Yet his explanation of why he prefers calling a council to acting on his own is somewhat disingenuous. Xenophon tells us that Cyrus in fact wanted this measure to be voted on "for the sake of the peers themselves, because he thought that they too would be better if they themselves were to be judged by their deeds and also to receive what they merited" (2.2.21). For all Chrysantas's talk of individual merit, even the peers, it seems, are not altogether against or innocent

15. Cf. 1.5.9; Aristotle *Politics* 1280a9–13.
16. *CL* 7.3.
17. Plato *Laws* 752a.

of enjoying certain undeserved benefits themselves. Indeed, as Cyrus learned at an early age, the tension or conflict between individual and collective benefits arises as a consequence of the Persians' devotion to justice, understood as the rule of law (1.3.17). This consideration also serves to remind us of another reason why Cyrus does not wish to institute this policy himself. To give the commoners an equal share, even if for equal work, would, strictly speaking, be a violation of Persian law, which unambiguously states that honors and rule, to say nothing of weapons for fighting at close quarters, are to go only to those who complete the full course of education (1.2.15). And if Cyrus does his best to instruct the new recruits in the rudiments of tactics, he makes no similar effort with justice, moderation, and the other Persian virtues. Should some strict defender of a literal interpretation of the law object to the questionable legality of this and other reforms, Cyrus could, of course, defend himself as one of those "most just and most law-abiding men" who step outside the established legal order only to lend it greater support. Even his father, the king and high priest of the Persians, admits that extralegal acts are sometimes necessary, especially in times of war (1.6.27). Moreover, Cyrus's democratic reforms appear to lead to the fulfillment of the unattained intent of the law to achieve equality, which was apparently thwarted only by economic scarcity (1.3.17–18; 1.2.15; 2.1.10–14).[18] They also seem to further the highest aim of the regime, which is to make all its citizens the best (1.2.15). If Cyrus acts by a standard that transcends mere legality, he does so while seeming to remain true to the spirit of justice on which the laws are founded.[19] But insofar as this justice is translegal, it also appears to be trans-Persian. The principles that allow them to open their ranks to the commoners make it possible to extend this invitation to good and useful men wherever they may be. As Plato's Socrates makes much more explicit, the concern with virtue and merit, although rooted in

18. For equality as the underlying aim of all good laws, see Herodotus 1.196 with 1.198. Cf. Thucydides 6.38–39; Aristotle *Politics* 1295b23–27.

19. In book 2, the section of the *Cyropaedia* devoted to the transformation of the Persian army, the terms for "justice" and its derivatives occur with relatively high frequency (seventeen times), whereas those for "law" and "the legal" (νόμος, νόμιμα) are found only in the mouth of Aglaitadas, the sole peer to criticize Cyrus's reforms explicitly. The same observation holds true for "moderation" (σωφροσύνη) and its related terms (2.2.14). Although among the relatively few named characters in the *Cyropaedia*, Aglaitadas does not appear again in the narrative.

what is otherwise a closed, conservative regime, contains the seeds of a potentially revolutionary, cosmopolitan idealism.[20] Accordingly, Cyrus now exhorts the Persians to fill their ranks with those who will contribute to their strength and honor regardless of their ethnic origins. He asks them to apply to politics the experience of sub- or suprapolitical concerns:

> Do not, however, think to fill out your ranks again [only] with citizens, but just as you seek whatever horses may be best, and not only those from your fatherland (πατριῶται), so also take from anywhere such human beings as you think will most contribute to your strength and good order. And what follows shows that what [I say] is for the good. Surely, a chariot could never be fast with slow horses, nor just with the unjust in the yoke; nor would a household be well managed if it used base servants, but it would suffer less by having no servants than unjust ones. (2.2.26)[21]

So far is the justice that will unite these disparate peoples from obedience to the law, or anything else taught in the Persian schools, that Cyrus can even speak of horses as possessing it.[22]

We must not forget, however, that a true open-door policy allows for both arrivals and departures (2.2.27; 6.2.36; 8.4.4). Perhaps again "for the sake of the peers," Cyrus is especially concerned to make use of the latter possibility. For whereas Chrysantas considers it the greatest inequality for good and bad to share alike, Cyrus fears something much worse, that is, for the bad actually to get more than the good. Those who are useless, like drones, merely burden their companions with the cost of their keep; but those who are vicious and eager to take advantage without toil may actually lead others into vice, and not without good reason: "For often they can demonstrate that vice does get the advantage" (2.2.24). Once virtue is no longer understood to be its own reward, remuneration will apparently not ensure its practice in the absence of an assiduous care to punish vice.[23] Such men must therefore be weeded out entirely.

---

20. Plato *Republic* 334c–335d.
21. Cf. *Poroi* 2.5–7.
22. Cf. *Oec.* 11.4–6, for the insight into human virtue that Socrates gains from his study of horses.
23. Cf. *CL* 9.4–6.

As promised, Cyrus assembles the army as a whole the next day in order to deliberate on the question of equal shares. With the peers he could speak openly of the dangerous power that vice has "often to get more." The peers' long habituation to virtue, and perhaps also the fact that vice might not succeed so well in the preservation of what has already been gained, makes such frankness possible.[24] No such admission is made before the commoners, who are, after all, focused solely on acquisition. Cyrus begins instead by reminding them of the approaching enemy and argues that the army will stand or fall as a whole. Finally, he evokes the threat of divinely sanctioned punishments: "The god has ordered things something like this: for those who are unwilling themselves to toil for the good things, the god sets up others to command them"(2.3.4). Cyrus then frames the issue to be debated: "Now, then, let anyone stand up and discuss whether he thinks virtue will be more practiced among us if the one willing to toil and run risks the most will also receive the most honor, or [will it be practiced more] if we know that all receive the same share, even the bad"(2.3.5). As if this prologue were not enough to suppress genuine debate, Chrysantas then rises to say that he believes Cyrus has introduced this question not as a matter for deliberation but as a test. He wants to see whether anyone is willing to let it be known that he thinks himself worthy of an equal share of what is gained by the virtue of others even if he does nothing good or noble himself. This peer, who on the previous day was complaining about the prospect of sharing equally with lesser men, now presents himself as a poor soldier, the least worthy of the peers, yet one prudent enough to be satisfied with a smaller share than his betters, if only to avoid having a larger share of defeat. Indeed, his appearance seems to bear out the truth of his speech, inasmuch as Xenophon tells us here that he was "a man neither tall nor strong to look at"(2.3.5; cf. 8.4.20).[25]

Cyrus may intimidate and shame the commoners into support for a strict meritocracy, but such coerced consent is hardly a sound basis for the kind of willing cooperation that his long-term project requires. Fortunately, one of the commoners stands up to speak in favor of the

24. Plato *Republic* 351c.
25. This appearance does not stop Cyrus from singling out Chrysantas after the first battle for special honor as "a mighty man of war" (4.1.4).

measure himself. Unlike Cyrus or Chrysantas, Pheraulus can hardly be suspected by the commoners of acting in the class interest of the peers.[26] Moreover, his stated motives and rhetoric are anything but obsequious. He neither mentions the common good nor expresses any concern about the survival of the army, or even the Persian regime. Instead, he exhorts his comrades to regard this measure as a challenge "to a contest in virtue" with the peers (τὸ ἀγωνίζεσθαι περὶ ἀρετῆς), one in which they will at last have the opportunity to compete on equal terms. All now take the same exercise and receive the same rations, all are considered worthy to associate together, the same prizes are set before all, and obedience to the rulers is required of everyone. Above all, to be brave in battle is prescribed as the noblest thing for each alike (2.3.8). If some of his comrades were left unpersuaded by Cyrus's earlier claim that fighting with a short sword and shield requires little skill (2.1.6), Pheraulus provides another reason for them to adopt these weapons with enthusiasm. Just as animals fight in various ways learned from no other source than nature (παρὰ τῆς φύσεως), now the commoners have placed before them those weapons that all human beings know by nature how to use (πάντες ἄνθρωποι φύσει ἐπιστάμενοι). To prove this point he cites his own untutored experience:

For instance, the bull strikes with his horns, the horse with his hoofs, the dog with his teeth, and the boar with his tusk. All of them also know how to guard against what they most need to, even though they have never frequented any teacher. As for myself, from childhood on, I knew how to protect myself by fending off blows from where I thought they would land. And if I had nothing else, I put out my hands to hinder the one hitting me. I did not do this because I had been taught; indeed, I was beaten for just this fending off. Moreover, even as a boy I used to grab a sword whenever I saw one, although I did not, I declare, learn how one must handle it from anyone other than nature. I did this not because I was taught, but even when I was kept from it, just as there were other things I was compelled to do by nature, despite both my mother and father hindering me [from doing them]. And, by Zeus, I used to hack with a sword everything that I could without getting caught. For

26. Xenophon, however, lets his readers know that this Pheraulus "was somehow well acquainted with Cyrus even when back at home in Persia" (2.3.7; cf. 8.3.37), and, later, that he was "not unconcerned with gratifying [Cyrus]"(8.3.5).

not only was this according to nature, like walking and running, but it seemed to me in addition to be pleasant as well as natural. (2.3.9–10)

What Pheraulus understands by nature is the spontaneous, that which he was not explicitly taught (or at least does not recall being taught) by others but still desired to do despite the risk of punishment.[27] In his view, success in battle depends then less on skill or art than on being spirited enough to overcome the fear of punishment by men and to do what nature teaches (2.3.12). And what he wanted to do most of all as a child, and apparently still desires as an adult, is to hack things to pieces with a sword.[28] By claiming that nature teaches all there is to know about fighting, Pheraulus manages to reduce the peers' education, much as Cyrus has already done (1.5.12), to training in the endurance of hunger, thirst, and cold. He can then draw an additional advantage from this premise: it is precisely in these matters that the commoners excel because they have received their instruction not merely at the hands of men but from necessity, "the best teacher of such things" (2.3.13). The peers may have accustomed themselves to toil by carrying arms, but Pheraulus and the commoners consider these "to have been discovered by all men to be the easiest things to carry." For them, carrying arms seems more like having wings than a burden. If Pheraulus begins his speech by encouraging the commoners to contend with the peers on the new basis of equality, he concludes by exhorting them to take advantage of their decisive superiority. Now that they have the upper hand, he claims, they should make the most of their advantage and "hasten into the strife of battle with these here who have been educated. For now these men have been trapped into a struggle with the common element" (2.3.15; cf. 1.5.11). Needless to say, the commoners adopt the proposal, after hearing "many others" speak in its support.[29] Cyrus, for his part, takes Pheraulus's suggestion to

27. For a similar, and similarly comic, view of nature, see Herodotus 2.2.
28. Cf. Plato *Republic* 359b.
29. In all of classical literature it is difficult to find a more sympathetic portrait of the plight and potential of the exploited classes. That we should find it in the pages of a book written by an author whose views are routinely considered to be nothing more than an expression of oligarchic class prejudices only confirms the need to reconsider Xenophon's reputation. For Xenophon's "liberal" and even "radical" views of women and his remarkable freedom from "gender" prejudices, see Pomeroy 1994, 36, 60.

heart and immediately sets about tapping the commoners' resentment by holding mock battles between the troops. He institutionalizes class strife in such a way as to accustom them to their new mode of fighting, increase their strength, and bring their spirit to a fever pitch (3.3.10; 3.3.57). Yet neither the acceptance of rewards based on merit nor the open appeal to class antagonisms are the most important results of this meeting.

Pheraulus appeals to both what is natural and what is pleasant but is careful to distinguish between the two, as must anyone who identifies the life according to nature with the life of a hoplite.[30] He knows a soldier's life is often filled with painful toil. Nature and pleasure may sometimes converge, as in the case of the undetected (or, at least, unpunished) hacking of things to pieces, but this is not always so. Pheraulus himself admits that the natural compulsion he felt to ward off blows often resulted in an even worse beating, to say nothing of the punishments he received for doing the other natural things to which he alludes, which were likewise against the wishes of his parents. His argument from nature might persuade the commoners to regard themselves as capable soldiers, but it does not necessarily have the force to make them take up arms and fight, especially when they know that should they choose to indulge this particular natural passion, there are enemies ready nearby to take the place of punishing parents. Nature may prepare all men for this way of life, but nature by itself does not make such a life choice-worthy in all circumstances. Some kind of supplement is required to make them willing to follow nature and fight as hoplites. In Pheraulus's case, this supplement is honor, and, according to him, "a life of honor is alone most pleasant"(2.3.11). But as Pheraulus knows only too well from his life back in Persia, honor is sometimes granted by men moved less by honorable motives than by prejudice, self-interest, and envy. To live wholeheartedly for honor requires belief in the existence of a powerful, unbiased judge

---

Delebecque 1978, 595, also remarks: "Dans toute son oeuvre, Xénophon manifeste une parfaite délicatesse envers les femmes."

30. In keeping with this position and its implied deprecation of the arts, including the art of war, Pheraulus speaks of weapons as being "*discovered* to be the easiest things to carry," rather than designed or made that way.

who will distribute it appropriately. Thus Pheraulus is willing to enter this contest, to choose "the most pleasant way of life," and the one that accords with nature, only on the condition that Cyrus be the one to determine and distribute rewards. Cyrus, he believes, will judge "without envy" and honor him and the others "according to merit" because "he seems to love those he sees to be good no less than himself." Pheraulus's own eyes provide evidence of this admirable disposition: "I see Cyrus is more pleased to give things away than to keep them for himself" (2.3.12, 15). Yet given the limits of what the human eye can see, this may not be conclusive proof. Certainly, the reader, with Xenophon's help, has seen that Cyrus's generosity and benevolence are not so disinterested as Pheraulus appears to believe. Nonetheless, the debate concludes not only with the establishment of the rule of rewards commensurate with merit but also with acceptance of Cyrus as the supreme judge of commoners and "peers" alike.[31]

Xenophon maintains that the character of a regime derives from the character of its leading men (οἱ προστάται, 8.8.5; *Poroi* 1.1). We would, then, expect the reforms Cyrus effects to be reflected in the different human types who flourish and predominate within the old and new dispensations. Aglaitadas is the only peer to speak up for their former way of life and to question Cyrus's innovations. A most austere and sober man, he objects to the spirit of playful levity that reigns in Cyrus's camp and helps to facilitate the assimilation of the commoners.[32] Not laughter but tears, he believes, make men good:

For the one who contrives a laugh for his friends seems to me often to do things much less worthy than he who makes them weep. And if you calculate correctly, you too will discover that what I say is true. For fathers contrive moderation in their sons, and teachers good lessons in the boys, by making them weep, and the laws turn citizens to justice by making them weep. Would you be able to say that those who contrive a laugh benefit either our bodies or our souls by making them better suited for managing a household or the affairs of the city? (2.2.14)

31. That such an elevation was intended by Cyrus from the start is indicated by his repeated references to the "so-called peers" in his first conversation with Cyaxares (2.1.3, 9). Compare his aims with Agesilaus's more modest procedure in similar circumstances (*Hel.* 4.2.5).

32. Cf. Plato *Republic* 388c.

Aglaitadas defends the ancestral way of life out of a concern for virtue and the good of the city, not self-interest. But even he must smile a bit when another peer points out that his way of life causes him to treat his friends no differently than his enemies: he seems to wish to make both weep. Aglaitadas's brief, forced smile illuminates, if only for a moment, the almost inhuman severity of a regime whose loyal citizens must practice a kind of self-brutalization, one that requires them both to accept their beatings willingly and then to praise them out of gratitude (1.2.7, 1.6.33). This citizen of Persia is the very model of those harsh republicans satirized by Montesquieu, whose devotion to the regime resembles that of fanatical monks who love their order precisely because it so much afflicts them.[33] Pheraulus, on the other hand, represents the type of man who will flourish under the new order. He is the commoner who most resembles Cyrus, if in a sometimes comic manner, and, with the exception of Cyrus, his is the most dramatic change of station, from a poor subsistence farmer to a wealthy and trusted confident of the king (8.3.2, 36–38). True, he lacks the moderation and concern for justice for its own sake that are the hallmark of the Persian peer. Nor does he regard the beatings his parents administered with the same grateful eye as does Aglaitadas; like Cyrus, he appears to be entirely lacking in any attachment to or respect for the ancestral. Yet this freedom from ties to family or love of his native soil, and his devotion to the pursuit of personal wealth and honor, are qualities ideally suited to Cyrus's new cosmopolitan regime; they make him an eager soldier, one willing to fight, not so much in defense of the fatherland, as for its eventual expansion into an empire. Inasmuch as these passions seem to grow in the human soul independent and even in spite of education, Pheraulus appears to be a kind of being more natural than the austere republican citizen he replaces, and hence provides more reliable, or at least more readily available, material out of which to build an empire that will draw its energy and strength from the emancipation rather than the conquest of its subjects' passions.

---

33. Montesquieu, *Spirit of the Laws*, 5.2. Araspas, a Mede, speaks most forcefully of the harsh and particularly unreasonable character of the Persian laws (5.1.11).

Armenia

Cyrus's policy of generously honoring and gratifying those he sees to be outstanding soldiers, which earns him the goodwill and confidence of commoners like Pheraulus, to say nothing of the peers, creates something of a logistics problem. Although Cyaxares has borne the expense of arming the commoners and continues to pay for the Persian army's maintenance (2.1.10, 2.4.9), Cyrus runs through whatever funds he has brought with him long before the enemy arrives. He hesitates to ask Cyaxares for more money, because he knows his uncle's finances are already strained; instead, he proposes to augment the Medes' treasury by making an expedition against the Armenians, the only ally they had thought they could count on (2.1.6), but who have nonetheless taken advantage of the Assyrians' approach to hold back their forces and stop payment of the tribute they owe the Medes. Cyaxares is at a loss what to do: whether to compel the Armenians' contribution or to leave them alone for fear of pushing them from neutrality into the ranks of their enemies. Cyrus, however, thinks he knows a way to get the Armenian king to send his army, pay the tribute, and even make him "more a friend to us than he is now"(2.4.14). Borrowing the stratagem the Assyrian prince had used in making a surprise attack on Media during Cyrus's sojourn there (2.4.16–17; 1.4.17), he overwhelms the Armenian's forces, captures his wife and children fleeing with their valuables, and surrounds the king and his few remaining troops where they have taken refuge on a hill. Cyrus then sends a message, "Tell me, Armenian, do you wish to remain here and fight hunger and thirst or come down onto the plain and fight us?" The Armenian is at a loss what to do (ἀπορῶν). Cyrus then proposes an alternative: he can come down to stand trial before "him whom the god has granted to treat you as he wishes, even without a trial." Recognizing the hopelessness of further resistance, the Armenian descends. Cyrus immediately gathers the Medes, Persians, those of the Armenian nobility who have not fled, and the women and children to witness the trial. The presence of these natives is essential to Cyrus's plan, as he intends to convict the Armenian, not on the basis of some Persian or Median understanding of justice, but by the standard of his own conduct. The fear that some of these subjects may inform on him if he lies encourages the Armenian to tell the truth.

Cyrus begins his cross-examination by reminding the Armenian of his defeat by Astyages, and how on that account he had agreed to pay tribute and supply troops to the Medes. Why has he now broken his word? The Armenian replies that he was longing both to be free himself and to bequeath freedom to his children. Cyrus does not condemn this aspiration and even adds that "it is noble to fight in order never to become a slave." But the Armenian was not willing to fight, at least not against great odds, and the timing of his revolt showed that he hoped to acquire freedom without a struggle. This unwillingness to fight, combined with his earlier acquiescence in his subordination to the Medes, seems to confirm, at least in Cyrus's eyes, the appropriateness of his subjugation. Perhaps this explains why Cyrus feels no need to inquire into the origins or justice of the war by which the Medes established their supremacy (3.1.10; cf. 1.5.13; 2.4.13). Still, if the Armenian is a slave, it must be admitted that there are different degrees of servitude, because he himself possesses slaves won in battle, and others serve him as subordinate officers (cf. 3.3.15). What, Cyrus asks him, does he do with his slaves when they run away, or with officers when they make mistakes? He punishes them, of course, and puts to death those caught deserting to the enemy, his own intended crime. "So, Armenian, since this is your justice, what do you advise us to do?" The Armenian is once again at a loss, this time "whether to advise Cyrus to kill him or to teach him a course opposite to what he did himself" (3.1.11–14).

We, as readers, know that Cyrus has no intention of killing the Armenian, even if he deserves as much by his own standards. Cyrus's stated purpose for coming to Armenia is to make the king send his army and pay the much-needed tribute. But Cyrus has also expressed the intention or hope of making the Armenian "more of a friend to us than he is now" (2.4.14). Inasmuch as he is in a position to do whatever he wants with the Armenian, and what he does is bring him to trial, the trial must somehow serve this end. At first glance, this would appear to be impossible, because to exact the men and tribute, Cyrus must crush the Armenian's aspirations to freedom, and in doing so humiliate him before his people. As their ends are strictly opposed, there is no common good between them and therefore no possibility of genuine friendship. However, if Cyrus can make the Armenian believe he stands convicted by his own contradictory and unjust behavior, the offer of a pardon might plausibly constitute a benefit for which the guilty king ought to be grateful. This explains Cyrus's desire to minimize his own responsibility for the Armenian's plight by presenting himself as the mere executor of another's will, yet one who is at the same time somehow free to act also as an intercessor (3.1.6).

While the Armenian awaits Cyrus's judgment in aporetic silence, one of his sons interrupts the proceedings. "Tell me, Cyrus, since my father seems to be at a loss, shall I advise you what I think to be best for you [to do] with him?" This son, Tigranes, was known to Cyrus from his days in Media, where as children they used to hunt together. At that time, Tigranes had been the companion and admirer of "a certain sophist." On account of this association, Cyrus "desires very much" to hear him speak and "eagerly" commands him to disclose his mind (3.1 14). Commentators are nearly unanimous in identifying this sophist with Socrates, and Tigranes with Xenophon himself. There is certainly a striking resemblance between Socrates and the sophist with regard to their teachings and the manner of their deaths: both held that wrongdoing arises involuntarily from ignorance; and both are executed on a charge of corrupting (διαφθείρειν) the youth.[34] This accusation had been in circulation against Socrates at least since the appearance of Aristophanes' *Clouds*. There we see a father, Strepsiades, who sends his son to study with Socrates in the hope that he will then defend him in the law courts, and who is outraged when the son returns home having learned instead to beat him.[35] Here Xenophon responds to Aristophanes' indictment by presenting just such a student loyally coming to his father's defense in his moment of greatest need.

Inasmuch as the Armenian stands convicted by his own practice, Tigranes makes no attempt to prove his father's innocence. Instead, he argues that since "he has done wrong in everything" (πάντα

34. Lucioni 1949, 395; Delebecque 1957, 394–95; Bizos 1973, 1: xlii, 2: 5; Bruell 1987, 103; Tatum 1989, 135, 144; Due 1989, 77; Gera 1993, 91–93; Ferrari 1995, 274 n. 12. In the *Cyropaedia*, where Xenophon considers political life almost entirely in the light cast by its own standards, the philosopher appears as a sophist; from the point of view of politics, it is difficult to distinguish between the two (Plato *Meno* 92b–95a). Socrates returns the favor in the *Oeconomicus*, where he treats Cyrus the Great and Cyrus the Younger as one and the same person, i.e., he abstracts from the distinction of vital importance to political men, that between practical success and failure.

35. Aristophanes *Clouds* 93–118, 882–88, 1210–11, 1331–1474.

ἡμαρτηκέναι), he should be imitated in nothing. In other words, Tigranes' first line of defense entails a complete denial of the respectability and authority of his father. Cyrus, however, is unpersuaded and makes the sound response that in doing justice, he will least of all be imitating one who does wrong. After all, Cyrus maintains, the Armenian did not do wrong by punishing offenders but in doing wrong himself. Because Tigranes admits his father's guilt, Cyrus is able to turn the tables and point out that "according to your argument your father must be punished, if indeed it is just to punish the unjust" (3.1.15). Now by refuting Tigranes' first and most feeble line of argument, Cyrus would seem to admit that not to punish the Armenian, his own ultimate and apparently intended course of action,[36] would be unjust. He also appears to have walked into a trap. As we learn in the sequel, Tigranes has at his disposal the Socratic argument that since men do wrong out of ignorance, they do so unwillingly and deserve to be corrected through education. Justice does not demand retributive punishment of those who err, but understanding, and, when possible, improvement by instruction.[37] Yet Xenophon, in the person of Tigranes, is careful not to confront Cyrus with this most far-reaching and radical of Socrates' discoveries, or at least does not do so in a context that demands a direct response (3.1.38). While this argument may justify the pardon he intends for the Armenian, if Cyrus were to accept it, along with the necessary corollaries,[38] he would also set a precedent that calls into question his own ambitions and practices.[39] Moreover, it is by no means clear that Tigranes accepts the soundness of this principle; he still seems to hold his father responsible for the sophist's death and has apparently neither forgiven nor instructed him (3.1.40).[40] He therefore passes up this opportunity to excuse his father's misdeeds and prefers to return the argument more directly to a consideration of what Cyrus considers to be his own self-interest with regard to the coming war. If this hard-nosed strategy might seem to confirm a more serious charge leveled in the *Clouds*, namely, that Socrates and his

36. Tatum 1989, 136, 138.
37. Cf. *Mem.* 1.2.50; Plato *Apology* 25d–26a.
38. *Mem.* 1.2.50, 3.9.4–5, 4.6.6–8.
39. See, e.g., 1.4.2, 1.5.13, 7.5.21.
40. Tigranes' resistance to the sophist's teaching is in line with Xenophon's account of his own resistence to Socrates' advice. See *Mem.* 1.3.11–13; *Anab.* 3.1.4–8.

students are indifferent to the claims of justice,[41] it is one imposed on Tigranes by his loyalty to an admittedly unjust father (3.1.1). But it is also a strategy likely to appeal to Cyrus, because it allows him to do what he wants with the Armenian, as opposed to what might be considered just (3.1.15, 1.3.18), while at the same time appearing to indulge an appeal for mercy on the part of a dutiful son.

In order to save his father, Tigranes attempts to persuade Cyrus that human beings are "worth the most at the moment they have been caught being unjust." He does this by beginning from the vaguely Socratic proposition that "without moderation there is no benefit from any other virtue."[42] He argues that his father, having been thoroughly bested by Cyrus, has been cured of all imprudence and is therefore willing to obey, just as happens when one city is beaten by another and immediately stops fighting and submits. Tigranes thus equates moderation with prudence, which in turn counsels obedience to the stronger (3.1.16–19). The argument is obviously flawed. Quite apart from the unproven premise underlying the analogy —namely, that what is good for a city is good for a man—or the ambiguity as to whom such moderation is most beneficial, the conqueror or the conquered, Tigranes assumes what Cyrus and the Persians doubt: namely, that "moderation" is a "passion of the soul" (πάθημα τῆς ψυχῆς), which can be acquired immediately, and not something learned (μάθημα) over time by dint of practice. In Persia, moderation was taught to the young by having the example of the elders constantly before their eyes and by camping out on guard duty every night for ten years, to say nothing of the the beatings inflicted by their fathers (1.2.8–9, 14; 2.2.14). However, Cyrus is intrigued by Tigranes' suggestion that "knowing others to be better than themselves is sufficient to make human beings become moderate," that is, willing to obey their superiors, regardless of whether they believe themselves to be guilty of some injustice (3.1.20).[43] If true, such a disposition would seem to make the realization of Cyrus's ambitions much less difficult, and perhaps diminish the necessity of relying on force (cf. 1.6.8). Yet, here, too, there are reasons to doubt its credibility: as a youth, Cyrus's

41. Aristophanes *Clouds* 1148–53.
42. *Mem.*3.9.5.
43. Cf. Aristotle *Politics* 1284b29–34.

own experience of being inferior in horsemanship only served to push him to surpass others (1.4.5); and the Armenian king, although once thoroughly beaten by the Medes, later tried to violate their treaty.[44] Tigranes is thus forced to concede that the recognition of one's superiors must in fact be supplemented by punishment from those superiors (διδόναι δίκην) if it is to produce the kind of moderation useful to rulers (3.1.22).[45] This admission would seem to open the way to putting the king to death, but Tigranes makes the further and rather unusual claim that his father has already been punished, because nothing enslaves human beings more than the kind of strong fear he now feels. Cyrus does not doubt that such fear makes the Armenian disposed to obey at the moment, but he worries that if restored to power, he will once again become hubristic and cause trouble in the future.

Up until this point, Tigranes has simply been trying to save his father's life. If implicit in his appeal to Cyrus's self-interest is the suggestion that he might possibly continue to make use of the Armenian in some capacity, this in no way requires, nor has Tigranes mentioned, his restoration. But he follows Cyrus's cue and now makes the case that returning his father to the throne is in fact the best policy. Because Cyrus cannot rule Armenia himself, he will have to turn over its administration to others. Prudence requires him to build and garrison forts before leaving in order to prevent future rebellions. Yet these open signs of distrust will surely cause the new rulers to resent those who build and man them. There seems to be no alternative to being weak and despised or strong and hated. But his father, and only he, Tigranes argues, will be able to accept these measures:

Who could you now find whom you could gratify at this time more than my father? For if you now allow someone to live who has never been unjust to you, what gratitude do you think he will feel to you? And if you do not take away his children and wife, who will love you for this more than he who believes it fitting for them to be taken away? And do you know of anyone who would be more pained at not having the kingship of Armenia than us, and who would also owe you the most gratitude for receiving it [back]? (3.1.29–30)

44. Cf. *Mem.* 3.5.8.
45. Note also the πολλάκις in Tigranes' earlier formulation at 3.1.21. Cf. *Hel.* 6.3.11.

The feeble and even laughable character of this argument has not gone unremarked. Marcel Bizos exclaims, "Quelle étrange conception des moyens de se faire des amis."[46] The political potential of servants who bear such guilt-stained consciences strains credulity.[47] Tigranes is therefore careful to conclude with some more down-to-earth observations: Cyrus should bear in mind that the country will be held more peacefully if its customary ways and rulers are not changed; and no one could raise more troops and money than his father in the short period of time required.

Only after these final observations does Xenophon tell us that "Cyrus was excessively pleased as he listened, because he believed all that he [had] promised to do for Cyaxares would work out for him. For he remembered having said that he thought he would make [the Armenian] more of a friend than before" (3.1.31). Cyrus's response to Tigranes' speech indicates the considerations that win his approval. "If I gratify you in these matters, Armenian, tell me, how large an army will you send me, and how much money will you contribute to the war?"—questions he presses until he receives an exact account. Yet the manner in which he expresses himself, his repeated claim to be the mere instrument or executor, first of the will of a god and now, most preposterously, of the silent Armenian, reveals his awareness of the unresolved difficulty. Cyrus may wish to gain men's gratitude, and even more so their love, but these things can only be acquired by giving, or appearing to give, positive benefits. Merely abstaining from harm, no matter how much deserved, is not enough (1.6.11, 24; 8.4.8). The Armenian confirms this by his subsequent behavior.

When looking around for a strategic site on which to build his fort, Cyrus discovers that much of Armenia has been abandoned and left uncultivated because of frequent raids by the neighboring Chaldaeans. They hold a commanding position on heights from which they can plunder the Armenians with impunity. By means of a surprise attack, and aided by the Chaldaeans' expectation that the Armenian soldiers will run away as usual at the slightest resistance, Cyrus manages to drive them from their stronghold. He immediately sets to work to

46. Bizos 1973, 2: 9.
47. Cf. Gibbon 1994, 3: 437.

build a fort on the summit and sends for the Armenian king to come
and help with its construction. The Armenian is ecstatic. Revealing
the true depth of the gratitude he had earlier expressed to Cyrus for
having spared himself and his family and restored the throne to him,
he declares, "*now* we have clearly been saved as never before" and that
this good deed more than makes up for the money Cyrus has taken.
Indeed, the Armenian would have paid many times as much to see
the Chaldaeans driven from the heights. It is only after this success
that he declares himself to be in Cyrus's debt and his people proclaim
Cyrus their benefactor and a good man (3.2.14–16; 3.3.4).[48]

Although the Armenian assists in the attack and contributes to the
construction and supply of the new fort, Cyrus has no intention of
turning it over to him. Just as he has held back from treating the
Armenian the way the latter treated his slaves, he restrains the Armenian from doing to the Chaldaeans what they have done to him.
He tells his own men that he intends to leave behind a garrison of
Medes and Persians in the fort so that "necessity will compel both
[the Chaldaeans and Armenians] to be moderate toward us" (3.2.4).
He expects this moderation to take the form of their living in peace
with one another. By a stroke of good fortune, it happens that the
two countries can be of mutual benefit to each other. The Armenians
have fertile land, much of it uncultivated because of the Chaldaeans'
plundering. Cyrus proposes that the Chaldaeans now earn their living by tilling these fields, for which they will pay the usual rent. The
Armenians will do the same thing with the unused pasturage in Chaldaea. Both sides will profit, and the Chaldaeans will make even more
money than they did from raiding. Yet if both sides benefit from the
peace, there remains a kind of imbalance between the two. Instead
of being plundered, the Armenian king will now collect greater rev-
enues and acquire pastures for his herds: an unmixed gain. The Chaldaeans, on the other hand, although made wealthier, are compelled
to trade the more pleasant (or, at least, more customary to them) life
of raiding for one of labor in the fields. It hardly seems fair that the
Armenian king, as the result of an admitted act of injustice (3.2.15,
3.1.1), should benefit more than the Chaldaeans. Perhaps, though,

---

48. Cf. *Hel.* 7.3.12.

he suffers another kind of loss, one particular to him and entirely appropriate.

After the trial of the Armenian, Cyrus inquires into the whereabouts of the sophist whom Tigranes so much admires. Tigranes explains that his father has had him killed because he thought he was corrupting him (3.1.30).[49] The Armenian interrupts to justify his act. Just as husbands kill other men when they catch them having intercourse with their wives, because this deprives the husbands of their due love, he killed the sophist out of envy that he had made his son admire him more than he did his own father (3.1.39).[50] Cyrus considers the execution of the sophist to have been "an entirely human error," and he urges Tigranes to forgive his father. But this does not stop him from engaging in something of the same "crime" for which the sophist was killed: supplanting the father in Tigranes' eyes. Within three days of Cyrus's arrival, Tigranes no longer considers himself an Armenian and prefers the company of Cyrus to his fatherland (3.2.8).[51] Although the Armenian king volunteers to lead his country's army, Cyrus instead offers the post to Tigranes, who willingly accepts, never to return to his homeland. Herein lies a demonstration of Cyrus's greatest superiority to the other great figure in Xenophon's world. If Socrates could do whatever he wanted with any interlocutor in speech,[52] Cyrus can do whatever he wants in deed. The envy of fathers cannot keep him from his purposes. He comes to court as a judge, not a defendant. Or, when he does consent to stand trial, it is at one arranged to further his interests and over which he himself presides (5.5.12ff.).

The Chaldaeans, however, are unlikely to take much satisfaction in this loss suffered by the Armenian king. Both sides admit the peace will be unstable in the absence of a stronger third party to enforce it. Economic gains are not enough to extinguish their enmity. True, they ultimately do unite in the building of the fort; but this is for their common defense, by which they understand primarily defense against one another, not some common enemy.[53] The Chaldaeans in

49. Cf. *Mem.* 1.1.1.
50. *Mem.* 1.2.51–55; Plato *Apology* 37d–e.
51. Cf. *Anab.* 3.1.4.
52. *Mem.* 1.2.14.
53. Cf. 5.3.22–23.

particular are more likely to feel the disadvantages of this peace. They must now work for a living, although some among them who had long lived off the labor of others "neither knew how to work nor were capable of it for they were habituated to support themselves by war." The loss of the heights means the loss of their livelihood and way of life. No new order, however just or profitable, can satisfy those who benefited most under the old. Such men are bound to cause difficulties even, or especially, for the best regime. Yet Xenophon takes the trouble to inform us that despite this original reluctance and pessimism, the peace between Armenia and Chaldaea held even in his own day, well after the collapse of Cyrus's empire (3.2.24; 8.8). Perhaps the peace owes its durability to the subsequent practice of intermarriage between the two peoples (3.2.23).[54] But such a solution requires many years to bear fruit, and Xenophon is far from sanguine about the character of the goods produced by this institution.[55] More likely both sides benefited from Cyrus's ability, indeed, his eager desire, to make use of the recalcitrant Chaldaeans as mercenaries against the Assyrians (3.2.26). The peace, then, owes its original stability only to the existence of a larger war. Now in many respects the position of these Chaldaean warriors is not unlike that of the Persian peers (3.2.25; 1.5.9, 11; 2.1.3, 14; 1.2.15). By showing what the two groups have in common, Xenophon compels us to wonder just how Cyrus plans to satisfy or handle them once his conquests come to an end. The Armenian expedition gives us a glimpse of the difficulties he will have to surmount in order to realize his own desire to be praised and loved by all men as their universal benefactor, a challenge more difficult to overcome than the envy of neglected or forgotten fathers.

54. Cf. Aristotle *Politics* 1280b35–39.

55. Consider the implied distinction between different kinds of wives at 7.5.60, not to mention the qualities that distinguish wives and concubines at 4.3.1; cf. *Symp.* 2.9–10. Consider also Ischomachus's expectations in the *Oeconomicus* with their likely outcome in Andocides *On the Mysteries* 124–27. Strauss 1970, 157. The results of marriage are particularly difficult to foresee. In having him join Hystaspas to Gobryas's daughter, Xenophon makes Cyrus in part responsible for the birth of Darius, the Persian who will ultimately supplant his own dynastic line (8.4.25–26). See 5.2.7 for the "anachronistic" use of "darics" in connection with Gobryas's daughter. For the benefits and limitations of intermarriage, see *Hel.* 5.2.19.

Cyaxares

The manner in which Cyrus evades the envy of Cyaxares, his uncle and nominal superior in command, is a masterpiece of political manipulation. We noted earlier that Cyrus was very pleased with the outcome of the Armenian affair "because he believed that everything he promised Cyaxares to do would work out for him. For he thought he would make [the Armenian] more of a friend than before" (3.1.31). A world of ambiguity lies in this brief account of Cyrus's private thoughts. How can he achieve this ambition when the Persians' and Medes' need for troops and tribute and the Armenian's longing for freedom are irreconcilably opposed, thus making it impossible for them to share in a genuine common good? Perhaps to make someone "more of a friend than before" does not necessarily require him to become a true friend; simply to have made him less of an enemy will suffice. A more troubling ambiguity emerges when we compare what Cyrus remembers saying to his uncle to what he actually said. His original statement to Cyaxares was, "I hope he [the Armenian] will become more a friend to us than he is now" (2.4.14). What drops out of Cyrus's later deliberation is the plural pronoun, "to us" (ἡμῖν). Its place is taken by the singular pronoun found in the previous sentence, "he believed that everything he promised Cyaxares to do would work out for him (αὐτῷ)." The antecedent of this pronoun is left unclear: is Cyrus pleased because he thinks things will work out for himself or for Cyaxares?[56] There is some evidence to indicate that a dutiful care for what benefits his uncle is what motivates him. Upon his return to Media, Cyrus sends the Armenian troops and tribute directly to Cyaxares (3.3.5). Still, it is also true that Cyrus goes out of his way to refuse the extra gold the Armenian's wife tries to give him, gallantly telling her and the assembled crowd, "You will not make me go around doing good deeds for pay" (3.3.3).[57] This sentiment would appear to be unobjectionable did not Xenophon's comment on this policy cast Cyrus's motives in a somewhat different light: "Thus Cyrus returned, not only enriched with the money he took, but he had also secured by his character much

56. See 7.5.37 with 7.5.42–47 and 8.3.2 with 8.3.5 for similarly revealing contrasts between Cyrus's private thoughts and public speeches.
57. Cf. 3.1.33–34, 1.5.9, 4.2.46, and esp. 6.1.26.

more than this that could be drawn upon when it might be needed"
(3.3.5).[58] The "much more than this" of which Xenophon speaks could
refer to the reputation this act of self-restraint earns for him, simply
to more money, or to both. In any case, Cyrus's "generosity" to the
Armenian's wife allows him to avoid giving or sharing this extra gold
with Cyaxares and leaves him free to take it all at some future date.
If this particular incident still allows room for some ambiguity in our
understanding of Cyrus's relation with his uncle, all doubts are dis-
pelled by his conduct over the course of the first two battles with the
Assyrians.

Despite the loan he takes from the Armenian and Cyaxares' continued contribution to the support of the Persian army (3.1.34; 3.3.14, 20),
Cyrus once again quickly runs through his own money by distributing
gifts to the most worthy of his troops. By this time, though, his soldiers
are ready to fight: their bodies have been toughened up, and they are
both familiar with their weapons and ready to submit to orders. Cyrus
also observes that his men are becoming envious of one another and
factious precisely on account of the many contests he has established.
He therefore decides to lead them against the enemy "as quickly as
possible"(3.3.10; cf. 1.6.26). Only the "common dangers" of war can
make them "friendly-minded" (φιλοφρόνως) toward one another and
unite them in the belief "that they are co-workers for the common
good." Only the near presence of the enemy can extinguish or control
the envy stirred up by the distribution of rewards commensurate with
merit. But when Cyrus makes the case to Cyaxares for bringing the war
to the Assyrians, his real concerns go unmentioned. As James Tatum
notes, Cyrus in fact "has two campaigns underway, only one of them
being against the Assyrian King."[59]

Cyrus begins making the case for an immediate attack on the
Assyrians by attributing to his uncle an embarrassed delicacy, one
that no doubt prevents Cyaxares from proposing the same course of
action for fear that the Persians will think his decision stems from
his displeasure at having to maintain them rather than from strategy.
Cyrus stresses the great cost of keeping the army idle in Media
and points out that if they were in the enemy's territory, they could

58. 4.2.10. Cf. *Oec.* 1.14.
59. Tatum 1989, 123.

support themselves by ravaging the countryside (cf. 1.6.17). Finally, he concludes: "[W]e shall employ soldiers with much better and stronger souls if we ourselves go against the enemy and do not seem to look upon them unwillingly . . . and my father always said, and you also say, and all others agree, that battles are won more by souls than by bodily strength" (3.3.15–19). Cyaxares may well believe this, but Cambyses never expressed such a view. In fact, he placed great stress on the need for a general to care for his men's bodies (1.6.10–17, 41). As for Cyrus, he seems to have taken at least an equal concern for his men's bodies and their souls (3.3.9), a position more in keeping with Xenophon's own views (3.3.59). Nonetheless, Cyaxares accepts his nephew's arguments and agrees to lead the army into enemy territory as soon as possible. As usual, Cyrus has his reasons for keeping his uncle in the dark, reasons that become fully manifest only in the aftermath of the first battle.

The army marches into Assyria, ravages the land, and takes a vast amount of booty. When the two opposing forces finally meet, the Persians and Medes manage to engage just a part of the more numerous Assyrian army and inflict such a defeat on them that the entire force retreats after nightfall in great confusion and disarray. Dawn breaks and the victors discover the Assyrians' flight and the many possessions left behind in the deserted camp. Cyrus is very eager to follow up the rout, but without the Medes' cavalry, the Persians are incapable of pursuit. He gathers his like-minded captains and together they go to Cyaxares to present their case.[60] Cyaxares opposes the plan. Xenophon tells us he did so out of envy that the proposal was not his own, and also because "it perhaps seemed well to him not to run further risks" (4.1.13). We must be careful here not to let the imputation of base motives too much color our evaluation of Cyaxares' position. Xenophon is a writer capable of putting sound arguments into the mouths of otherwise disreputable characters.[61] And Cyaxares' argument is essentially one of cautious moderation:

Cyrus, that you Persians take the noblest care not to be overly disposed toward any pleasure, I know from seeing and hearing. But it seems to me most especially advantageous to be continent in the greatest pleasure. And

60. See Tatum 1989, 118, 126–27, for the manner in which Cyrus conducts more and more of his business with Cyaxares in public settings.

61. E.g., 5.1.11 with 1.2.3; *Mem.* 1.2.12, 40–46.

what gives human beings a greater pleasure than the good fortune (εὐτυχία) that has now fallen to us? If then, when we enjoy good fortune, we guard it moderately, we might perhaps be able to grow old in happiness without risk. But if we are insatiable in this good fortune and try to pursue another and another [victory], see that we do not suffer what so many have suffered at sea, that is, to perish because they were not willing to stop sailing on account of their good fortune. And many others who chance upon one victory, throw it away in yearning for another. If our enemies fled because they were weaker than we, perhaps it might then be safe to pursue the weaker. But bear in mind now that we defeated just a fraction of them, although all of our forces fought while the rest of theirs did not. If we do not compel them to fight, they will remain unknowing, both of us and themselves, and go away owing to their softness and ignorance. But if they come to recognize that there is no less danger in running away than standing fast, beware that we compel them to become good, even if they do not wish to. For surely, you are not so eager to take their women and children as they are to save them. Consider that even wild sows flee with their young whenever they are discovered; but if anyone tries to capture one of her young, she no longer flees but charges the hunter, even if she happens to be alone. And when they locked themselves up inside their fortifications and gave themselves to us to be counted out, this allowed us to fight with as many of them as we wished. But if we meet them on the plain and they learn to face us in separate detachments—some in front, as just now, but others from the side and behind—see to it that we do not, each one of us, stand in need of many hands and eyes. (4.1.14–18)[62]

There is nothing false in this argument and nothing that would not readily be seconded by Cyrus's father, Cambyses.[63] Events will prove that the risks of pursuit are much greater than even those Cyaxares foresees. But the Mede cannot leave well enough alone. Conscious of his own love of pleasure and shamed by the impressive austerity

62. Cf. Machiavelli, *Discourses*, 3.12.
63. Cf. 1.6.26, 44–46. Gera 1993, 105, comments: "Commonplace or not, Cyaxares' words are not ridiculous and the stance he assumes here is a legitimate one: this is one of the rare instances where the author of the *Cyropaedia* allows us to see that serious, worthwhile objections can be made to a proposal put forward by Cyrus." Gera ascribes a kind of clumsiness on the part of Xenophon for putting sober advice in the mouth of a character usually presented as "peevish." She is, however, unaware of the reasons why Cyrus must continue the war at any cost, and hence why Xenophon might wish to avoid stressing just how questionable, both morally and militarily, his plan has been from the very beginning. Consider 6.1.12, where, with typical exaggeration, Cyrus characterizes the amount of time in which the Assyrians could replace the fallen with a new generation of warriors as "very quickly."

of the Persians, Cyaxares concludes by taking refuge in the alleged disposition of his men: "Besides, now that I see the Medes enjoying themselves, I should not like to rouse them up and compel them to go into danger" (4.1.18). This pretense, the tribute vice pays to what it takes to be virtue, opens up the smallest of gaps, through which Cyrus is then able to push his more ambitious scheme.

Cyrus does not dispute his uncle's assessment of the military situation, although this would certainly have been one way to press for further action. He is careful to say nothing to indicate that he does not share his commander's views. He agrees that the Assyrian threat has been eliminated and that his official mission has therefore come to a successful close. Yet while he spoke with some bitterness to his captains of how the Persians' lack of cavalry prevents them from pursuing the Assyrians' main force, he assures Cyaxares that if he lends the Persians some horsemen, they will certainly not pursue the main body of the enemy but will only round up stragglers (4.1.11, 19). Cyrus appeals both to his uncle's greed and to his sense of shame: it would be terribly ungenerous for him to refuse to do something for those who have traveled such a long way to help. "So it is just that you now gratify us in return, so that we may go home with something and not always be looking to your treasury" (4.1.20). Cyrus misleads Cyaxares about his going home, as if this were his ultimate destination. In fact, a return to Persia is no longer a viable option. Having armed 30,000 commoners and given them basic military training, to say nothing of transforming the peers' understanding of virtue, Cyrus could not go back to Persia without destroying the balance of power between the classes there that gives the Persian regime much of its shape and stability. This realization puts us in a better position to understand Cyrus's desire to keep Cyaxares ignorant of the domestic political situation in Persia, his eagerness to engage the Assyrians "as quickly as possible," and also his reluctance to disclose the real cause of that eagerness. It is worth noting that had the Assyrian king decided to call off his expedition in the face of the allies' preparations, Cyrus would have been forced to become the aggressor, not only in fact, as it turns out he is, but in the eyes of his followers as well (3.3.22–23, 44; 4.3.12; 1.5.13). Whether his men realize it yet or not, he has from the time of his first address to the peers put the Persians on a course that they must follow to the end or fail. He now has no choice but to conquer or suffer the dire consequences of his yet incomplete reforms.[64] Ignorant of the necessities Cyrus has created, and believing that very few of his own men will respond to the call, Cyaxares allows him to select a messenger to announce to the Medes that those who are willing may go along with the Persians to hunt down any stragglers. Cyrus makes the most of this opportunity and sends Artabazus, a Mede who had fallen passionately in love with him during his earlier stay at his grandfather's court (4.1.22–23; 1.4.27–28).[65] The soundness of this choice is confirmed when Artabazus manages to persuade "nearly all of the Medes, except those who happened to be feasting in the tent with Cyaxares" to follow Cyrus (4.2.11).

The number of Medes willing to continue the fight also increases when it becomes known to them that messengers have come "in some divine way" (θείως πως) from the Hyrcanians, a people subject to the Assyrians and renowned for their horsemanship. Xenophon goes on to give an account of their providential arrival entirely in human terms. The Assyrians use the Hyrcanians much as the Lacedaemonians did the Sciritae, "sparing them in neither toils nor dangers." When the Hyrcanians reflect on what they have suffered at the hands of their Assyrian masters, the recent defeat and death of the Assyrian king, the panic in the army, the flight of many of his other allies, and on themselves being placed at the rear of the retreat, "so that if anything terrible should come they would get it first," they decide to defect to Cyrus and offer him their services as guides.[66] Cyrus, who knows nothing of these wrongs and makes no inquiry into their motives, accepts the Hyrcanians as allies, although in doing so he seems to abet the same crime for which he not long ago convicted the Armenian. His agreement to the terms of their assistance also constitutes a violation of the terms on which he has borrowed Cyaxares' cavalry (4.2.4, 8, 12; 4.1.19; 5.1.21–22; 6.1.7). It should come as no

64. Cf. Thucydides 3.27–28 for a foreseeable complication of arming commoners.

65. Artabazus is not formally named until much later in the book, at 6.1.9, although Xenophon clearly identifies him as the same Mede who was in love with Cyrus from his youth. For Xenophon's technique of withholding and granting proper names to characters, see Tatum 1989, 164–65, 175–77.

66. Compare his similarly human explanation of the origin of the belief that Cyrus is "descended from the gods" at 4.1.24. Xenophon's reputation as a conventionally pious Greek is exaggerated, to say the least.

great surprise that Cyrus fails to alert Cyaxares of this unexpected development.

With the decisive help of these new allies, Cyrus pursues, attacks, and conquers the "main body" of the enemy almost without a fight (4.2.19, 28). The importance of this additional victory, whose most significant result turns out to be the capture of 2,000 horse, is underlined by the astonishing risks Cyrus runs to secure it. First, if the Hyrcanian deserters take Cyrus's confident adoption of their cause to be a manifestation of "his strength of soul," we, as readers, are aware that he has no choice but to trust in their good faith. There is not even time to receive hostages from them as surety for their promises, a precaution Cyrus is careful to take when no longer in such desperate straits (4.2.7, 13, 20; 5.2.14–15). Second, his tactics have left the Persian army dangerously exposed in the aftermath of the rout (4.3.5). And, last, he knowingly marches out in pursuit of the Assyrians without provisions, perhaps the most fundamental error a general can commit, and one whose magnitude Xenophon stresses by remarking here in his own name "that without [food and drink] it is not possible either to campaign or do anything else" (4.2.34; cf. 6.2.26).[67] Again, Cyrus runs these risks and commits these manifest "blunders," not out of ignorance, but because the situation he has created makes them necessary. For him, in contrast to Cyaxares, anything less than the complete conquest of the Assyrian empire would amount to a defeat. However, had the untested Hyrcanians played Cyrus false, the initial victory over the Assyrian could have easily been reversed and Cyaxares' good judgment fully vindicated.

The next morning, Cyaxares emerges from his tent to find the camp deserted. Furious at having been left alone and exposed to great danger, he immediately dispatches a messenger to rebuke Cyrus and to command the Medes to return to him. When informed of the Hyrcanian defection, a development that Cyrus had somehow failed to report, he becomes even more incensed and revises his orders to

---

67. Cambyses takes special care to warn Cyrus against this risk, "You doubtless know that if the army does not have the necessities, your rule will dissolve at once.... Above all else, remember never to wait to provide supplies until need compels you; but when you are especially well off, then contrive to provide them before you are in need" (1.6.9–10; cf. *Hel.* 7.2.18). Compare Cyrus's actions at 4.2.19–34 with his promise at 1.6.11.

include much harsher threats (4.5.8–12). The envoy finally catches up with Cyrus several days later and delivers Cyaxares' message before the assembled allies. The Medes, struck dumb with fear, are at a loss how not to obey their ruler's unambiguous command. At the same time they are unwilling to return, because they have had firsthand experience of Cyaxares' savage wrath. As for the Persians, they know that the Median cavalry forms an integral and, at the moment, irreplaceable part of Cyrus's force. Were the Medes to obey, it is the Persians and Hyrcanians who would truly be at a loss (4.5.23). Cyrus intervenes at this delicate juncture to soften and deflect the force of Cyaxares' letter by offering his own (re)interpretation of its contents:

> I am not at all amazed, messenger and Medes, if Cyaxares is concerned both for himself and us, after having seen so many enemies and not knowing how we fare. But when he perceives that many of the enemy have been destroyed, and that all have been driven away, he will first stop being afraid and then recognize that he is not now abandoned, because his friends are destroying his enemies. Furthermore, how do we, who are doing him good, deserve blame, when even this we did not do on our own initiative? Indeed, I persuaded him to let me take you out. It's not as though you were eager or asked to go on this expedition; whoever among you was not averse to it, you came after having been ordered to do so by him. His anger, I am certain, will then be assuaged by our deeds, and will cease with the passing of his fear. (4.5.20–21)

Of course, Cyaxares makes no mention in the message of his fear, nor does he express any concern about the safety of Cyrus and the Medes. And, more important, at no point has he ever "ordered" anyone to follow Cyrus.[68] Despite or because of this gross misreading of the letter, the Medes are reassured and make no move to rejoin their king. Cyrus does his best to delay the return of the envoy and arranges to send one of his own with a message for Cyaxares (4.5.25, 4.6.12). This letter he contrives to read out loud before sending it, in order to allay whatever residual worry the Medes may harbor for having disobeyed their king's explicit command. It also serves to secure their attachment to himself. Cyrus regrets to inform Cyaxares that his recall of the Medes at a point when the army finds itself in a hostile territory now "compels me to forget you, although before I thought I owed you a debt of gratitude, and instead I must try and repay all my gratitude

---

68. Cf. 5.1.25, 5.5.22.

to those who [have] followed me." There is no mention of returning the cavalry as Cyaxares has explicitly ordered, just a vague promise that "we shall try to be with you as soon as we have accomplished what we believe will be common goods for you and us." Although Cyrus has himself just committed and continues to commit the offense that he accuses Cyaxares merely of intending—that is, leaving an ally defenseless and exposed in enemy territory—he maintains that his behavior is altogether different and above reproach: "I, however, am not able to be like you. At the moment I am sending to Persia for [another] army and command that if you have any need of them before they come to us, they will be at your disposal" (4.5.30–31). This offer is nothing if not insulting. In exchange for not sending back the borrowed cavalry as Cyaxares has ordered, Cyrus grants the future use of an unspecified force, which may or may not be forthcoming. Moreover, we recall (as must Cyaxares), that at the beginning of the war and when the situation appeared most critical, Cyrus refused to send for a larger army as something altogether impractical (2.1.8). But at least since the time of the Armenian expedition, he has himself been contemplating just such a measure (3.2.29). Indeed, in the time between the arrival of Cyaxares' envoy and the public announcement of his message, Cyrus has already summoned the peers to a meeting at which they have agreed to send home for reinforcements. This was not done with a view to succoring Cyaxares or to recompensing him for the loss of his cavalry, but in order to have sufficient troops to guard their captured spoils and to assure themselves of "rule over Asia and its fruits"(4.5.15–16). Needless to say, by the time these troops arrive, Cyaxares can neither use nor maintain them, and he immediately sends them on to Cyrus (5.5.3–4). But the most galling section of the letter to be read out loud is its conclusion, in which Cyrus takes it upon himself to give his uncle some belated if well-timed instruction on how best to manage his own men: "Even though I am younger, I advise you not to take back what you give in order not to reap enmity instead of gratitude. When you wish someone to come to you quickly, do not summon him with threats; and when you assert that you are alone, do not threaten those who are many, lest you teach them to think nothing of you. We, however, shall try to come as soon as we have accomplished what we believe will be, when done, common goods for both you and us" (4.5.32–33). Implicit in Cyrus's calm statement of the difference in strength between "us" (we Persians, Medes, Armenians, Chaldaeans, and Hyrcanians) and "you" (the singular σοί, Cyaxares), is his willingness to take advantage of this imbalance. Quite apart from reminding Cyaxares of the actual state of affairs, the letter serves to teach all those who hear it "to think nothing" of its recipient. For this refusal to comply with Cyaxares' direct command assures the Medes that they will have nothing to fear from their king so long as they stick with Cyrus. But if the Medes are the principal audience for this reading, Cyrus must also keep in mind that there are other allies present in the audience. He is therefore careful to avoid an open breech with his uncle and still holds out the possibility of their sharing "common goods" in the future. Outright disobedience or the staging of an open coup might cast doubts on the justice of his dealings with Cyaxares and perhaps raise suspicions in the minds of his other allies about his reliability or their own ultimate fate.[69]

To avoid the appearance of any injustice toward his uncle and commander, Cyrus strives to effect a reconciliation when they do finally meet again. In the end, it is Cyaxares who comes to Cyrus (5.5.1, 42; cf. 4.5.33). His nephew goes out to meet him, displaying his newly acquired power. Since they last parted, Cyrus has captured three enemy forts and added the Cadusians and two important Assyrian defectors, Gobryas and Gadatas, to the ranks of the allies. If these were the kind of common goods he had in mind to acquire for them both, Cyaxares is far from pleased by his efforts. Looking from these assembled troops to his own small retinue, he is seized with grief, refuses to return Cyrus's greeting, and begins to weep. Cyrus orders all the others away and leads Cyaxares to the side of the road where they can sit down to discuss the situation in private. Cyaxares is incensed at having been humiliated before his men, to see "even my slaves coming out to meet me stronger and prepared to be able to do me more harm than they can suffer at my hands." Even worse is to have been put in this position, not by an enemy, but by a close relative and ally. Cyrus declines to defend (ἀπολογεῖσθαι) the Medes, on the grounds that this would only serve to increase Cyaxares' anger; but he insists on clearing his own name. Concerning his alleged disobedience, if he failed to return the Median troops when ordered, Cyrus claims he

69. Cf. *Anab.* 7.7.23–24.

did so for his uncle's own good. He feared they might be provoked by Cyaxares' indiscriminate wrath to commit some rash act (5.5.8–12). We note, however, that this solicitude for Cyaxares' well-being and protection from his own men is first mentioned here; nor did it earlier prevent Cyrus from leaving his uncle almost defenseless in the midst of enemy territory. But he is more intent on disproving the general charge of having treated Cyaxares unjustly (ἀδίκως) and accordingly neglects such details when he effectively puts himself on trial for that crime. In order that they not blame each other randomly, Cyrus insists they begin by specifying just what sort of injustice he is accused of. Deborah Gera points out that Cyrus's procedure here resembles the descriptions of Socrates' method of investigation found in the *Memorabilia*.[70] More precisely, Cyrus employs only "Odyssean" dialectics, of the kind by which Socrates established agreement among his listeners about a subject matter, but not the truth[71] For the truth is the last thing Cyrus wishes to emerge from this exchange with his uncle.

Cyrus begins by reminding Cyaxares that when asked by him to lead the Persian army, he did so and came with as many men as he was able to bring; and when they engaged the enemy, he spared neither labor nor risk. Cyaxares can only agree that these were both good deeds.[72] Cyrus goes on: "Furthermore, when, with [the help of] the gods, victory was ours, and the enemy had retreated, I called on you to pursue them in common so that we might take vengeance in common, and if anything noble and good resulted we might harvest it in common. Can you accuse me of taking unfair advantage (πλεονεξία) in this?"(5.5.19) Cyaxares responds with silence, but whether because he considers himself refuted or is simply stunned by the audacity of Cyrus's fabrication is far from clear. For at the time of the Assyrians' retreat, Cyrus had requested the Medes' cavalry only to chase down the stragglers, so that the Persians "might go home with something in our possession"(4.1.20). Cyrus takes advantage of this silence to shift from the defensive and accuse Cyaxares of having held back out of fear and an unwillingness to disturb the Medes in their celebration, a charge

70. Gera 1993, 101.
71. *Mem.* 4.6.14–15. Strauss 1972, 122–23.
72. Cf., however, 5.5.16 with 2.1.8 and 4.5.16.

with some basis in fact, but one that by no means reflects the strength of his real objections to the continued prosecution of the war. Cyrus claims that ever since the Persians and Medes left him behind, they have done nothing but good for Cyaxares, killing his enemies, enriching his men, and capturing forts. He leaves unmentioned that for which there is apparently no excuse: his failure to inform his superior of the Hyrcanians' defection, an offense that Cyaxares in his anger seems fortunately to have forgotten.

Even so, Cyaxares does mount an impressive response. He says that he would prefer to increase Cyrus's lands by his power than to have his own increased by that of Cyrus. The favors Cyrus renders somehow serve only to diminish and dishonor him.[73] He asks Cyrus to put himself in his place. If someone were to win over and alienate the affections of a man's dogs and servants, or, even worse, his wife's love, "would he delight you by this good deed?" (5.5.28–31). Cyaxares' accusation recalls that brought by the Armenian king against the sophist, and is expressed by means of a similar analogy. On that occasion, Cyrus considered the Armenian to have committed an entirely "human error" in executing the sophist and urged Tigranes to forgive his father (3.1.39–40). Would he consider it an equally human and forgivable error if Cyaxares were now to repay such "favors" with death? Much as the Armenian was found guilty by the standard of his own practice, Cyrus's tolerance, if not approval, of the Armenian's handling of the sophist's "corruption" of his son would seem to have set a dangerous precedent, one that might well encourage a similar tolerance for Cyaxares should he undertake to punish him for alienating the affections of the Medes. Indeed, the harm Cyrus inflicts on Cyaxares is in some ways much worse than what the sophist did to the Armenian. A father, though despised or neglected by a son, may continue to hold his position and exercise rule by means of physical or other constraints, and this with the approval and backing of the laws and customs of the community. But, as Cyaxares here points out, a ruler can never exceed his people in physical strength; his power therefore

73. See Aristotle *Politics* 1223a34–b17. In the same spirit, Gera remarks: "The regular scheme of values in the *Cyropaedia* does in fact pose a problem: for every happy benefactor there must be a humiliated recipient" (Gera 1993, 106). As we shall see in the following chapter, such humiliation is perhaps the least of the difficulties created by Cyrus's "scheme of values."

rests at bottom on their esteem, on the belief that he is somehow better than them in important respects. It is this esteem that Cyrus, while putatively serving his uncle, has in fact stolen (5.5.34). Cyaxares' anger may be entirely understandable; but this makes it all the more necessary to guard against it. Cyrus anticipates his victim's all-too-human inclination to take vengeance and, unlike the sophist, is careful to postpone the inevitable conflict until he is in a position to resist and deter retaliation (4.5.33; 5.5.1).

Cyrus interrupts before Cyaxares has finished. He may have the upper hand for the moment, but his position is not impregnable, because he, too, as a ruler, depends on his subjects' belief in his goodness and superiority, especially on their good opinion of his justice and benevolence (2.3.15; 4.2.38, 42; 5.1.6, 28; 8.1.40). Cyaxares' accusations are potentially quite dangerous. It is one thing to level such charges in the course of a private conversation, but were he to press his case in public, some might be shocked by the evidence of Cyrus's disloyalty and perhaps begin to form some premonition of what might await them in the future. Having nothing to respond to the facts of his uncle's case against him, Cyrus swears an oath and begs his uncle to stop blaming him, at least until he has clear proof of how he and the men are actually disposed toward him.[74] Although the charges stand unrefuted, Cyaxares relents and greets Cyrus with a kiss before the assembled troops. The two mount their horses and together take the lead, the Persians following behind Cyrus and the Medes behind Cyaxares, "for Cyrus gave them a nod to do so" (5.5.37). Once in the camp, the Medes present themselves to Cyaxares bearing gifts, some on their own but most after having been ordered to do so by Cyrus. "Consequently, Cyaxares changed his mind and did not think that Cyrus was leading a revolt or that the Medes were any less attentive to him" (5.5.40). From this moment on, Cyaxares is relegated to the margins of the conflict.[75]

The resolution of this conflict and the final reconciliation between the two men rests at bottom on Cyrus's ability to deceive, to persuade

74. Carlier, 1978, 147: "Cyrus ne trouve rien à repondre, il se content de réaffirmer son affection pour son oncle."

75. At 5.5.44, Cyrus quietly excludes Cyaxares from among his friends who are "most capable of thinking, and if necessary, of acting together." At 6.1.13, he likewise corrects the mistaken impression Cyaxares may have given the allies at 6.1.6.

his uncle to believe that his subjects' allegiance remains unaltered, and that what he does to advance his own interests and ambition is in fact done for their common good. Xenophon indicates the true nature of the relations between them most clearly, if indirectly, however, when he lists Media among the countries given by Cyrus to his younger son to rule over as a satrap (8.7.11). Satraps, we are elsewhere told, are sent to rule over conquered peoples (8.6.1).[76] The scope of Cyrus's deceptions, so intriguing to Machiavelli and astonishing to Montaigne,[77] goes beyond their use as means to an ascent and extends into the very fabric of his rule.[78] Although the conflict between Cyrus and Cyaxares hearkens back to Achilles' quarrel with Agamemnon,[79] the manner of its resolution is entirely Odyssean.[80] The *Cyropaedia* thus remains outside the range of tragedy.

Cavalry

Cyaxares' reluctance to follow up the initial victory over the Armenian makes him an obstacle to Cyrus's wider plans. If his desire to return home and "grow old in happiness" is respectable, the fact that he is also envious of those who come up with the proposal to pursue the war gives Cyrus a pretext and plausible justification for leaving this less ambitious ruler behind. The display that Cyrus makes of the Persian cavalry, the lack of which had formed the basis for their common enterprise with and dependence on the Medes, contributes to the ease with which he persuades Cyaxares not to press his accusations in public, to believe that his men remain loyal to him, and to agree to continue with the war (cf. 1.6.10). Yet the measures Cyrus takes to acquire this cavalry indicate that his relations even with those of the allies who eagerly join and willingly follow him are fraught with similar tensions.

76. Bruell 1969, 67. Gera 1993, 100, points out that "in this section of the *Cyropaedia* we are given, in fact, the strongest hints of the actual historical sequence of events—the conquest of the Median empire by Cyrus."

77. Machiavelli, *Discourses*, 2.13.1; Montaigne, *Essais*, 1.6.

78. Carlier 1978, 147: "Pour Xénophon, un conquérant est, au sens plein du terme, un séducteur."

79. Stadter 1991, 489.

80. *Mem.* 1.2.58–59, 4.6.15.

As the majority of the Assyrians escape with most of their goods after the first battle, it is not difficult for Cyrus to persuade the Persians and Medes to continue the fight, especially with the addition of the Hyrcanians to their forces. With the second victory, the Persians manage to capture the enemy camp and with it a large amount of spoils. But the greatest and most valuable things are tracked down and taken by the Median and Hyrcanian horse, who in the aftermath show themselves little inclined to recognize or obey Cyrus as their ruler (4.3.1–3). This situation so vexes Cyrus that he calls together his captains to deliberate on the matter and to persuade them of the necessity of acquiring their own cavalry. As matters stand, the Persian infantry has contributed the most to the defeat of their enemy; but the allies believe that the spoils belong no less to them, and perhaps even more so (4.3.6). Cyrus now admits that with all the Persians equipped for fighting at close quarters, the army is extremely vulnerable to the archers and spearmen of the enemy, who can attack from a distance without risk. Far from making the Persian army safer, as he had earlier maintained, his initial reform has in fact left it open to attack by light-armed troops (2.1.11–12; 4.3.5).[81] This result may well have been intended, for its effect is now to make the Persians more inclined to embrace what is an even more radical military reform. Cyrus does not propose restoring the army to its original form but suggests the addition of a new Persian force. "If we were to acquire a cavalry not inferior to theirs [the allies], is it not apparent to us all that we would be able to do to our enemies without them what we now do with them? And they [the allies] would also become more measured in their disposition toward us" (4.3.7).[82] Here before them are many horses captured from the enemy, horses that Cyrus has on his own initiative taken special care to keep guarded within the camp and therefore within the Persians' grasp (4.2.32; 4.5.36). All they lack are the men to ride them.

What the peers really lack are not simply men to ride, but men who know how to ride. Not even Cyrus is willing to claim that riding requires little skill or training, as he did when speaking to the commoners of the basic skills of infantry (3.3.50; 1.4.4; 2.1.6). Nor can he plausibly argue,

81. Cf. *Anab.* 7.6.28–30; *Hel.* 3.2.3–4; 4.5.13.
82. Cf. 3.2.4; *Hipparchicus* 5.13.

after the manner of Pheraulus, that men know how to ride by nature, especially because horses are almost unknown in Persia (1.3.3). He encourages the peers to take heart in the fact that "no one who knows how to ride did so before he learned." If someone should object that these others learned to ride as boys, Cyrus is ready with a series of counterarguments:

Are boys any more prudent at learning what is said and demonstrated than men? And to put into practice with bodily strength what they've learned, who are more competent, boys or men? And we have more leisure for learning than either boys or other men. For we do not need to learn how to shoot the bow, as do boys, because we already know this. Nor how to throw the spear, because we know this too. Unlike other men, we are not occupied some with farming, others with the arts or domestic affairs. For us there is not only leisure but also the necessity to continue campaigning. And surely [riding] is not like many other military [skills], difficult but useful. Is not riding on a journey more pleasant than marching on your own two feet? Is it not pleasant to reach a friend quickly when speed is required, or when hunting a man or beast to catch him quickly? And is it not convenient when under arms to have a horse share the burden? Certainly, to hold and to carry are not the same. Yet someone might be fearful if we were compelled to run risks on horseback before we had mastered the job. But even this [difficulty] is not insurmountable. For whenever we wish, we may at once fight on foot. And in learning how to ride, we shall not unlearn our infantry skills. (4.3.11–14)

These arguments are rather feeble and especially dubious in light of Cyrus's own opinion about the defects of "late learners" (3.3.37; cf. 1.6.35). But their significance pales in comparison with the importance of an observation he makes almost in passing. For the first time, he openly admits to the Persians the stark truth of their new situation. "For us there is not only leisure but also the necessity to continue campaigning," which is to say, strictly speaking, they have no leisure. But if their end is now irrevocably fixed by necessity, they can still consider themselves free to deliberate about the best means to achieve it. Cyrus concludes his speech with an unprecedented suggestion: he proposes that in order to encourage the attainment of good horsemanship, they make a law for themselves declaring it shameful to be seen going anywhere on foot, no matter how long or short the journey (4.3.22). With the sight of the allies before them riding in and out of the camp on horses laden with spoils, the peers vote unanimously in favor of the proposal, increasing their military